Growing up on the Banks of the *Mighty Tittabawassee*

– Kittie's Childhood Memoirs: 1891 to 1904 –

Revisit Freeland's historic past with Kittie! Ros Ederer

Freeland's History & Historical Notes
By
Roselynn Ederer

Childhood Memoirs & Line Drawings
By
Kathryn Ellen Lewis
"Kittie"

Published by Roselynn Ederer and Kathryn Ellen Lewis in cooperation with Thomastown Publishing Co., P.O. Box 6471, Saginaw, MI 48608-6471. Additional copies and volume discounts available. E-mail: Ttpublishing@aol.com

Publisher's Cataloging-in-Publication Data
Ederer, Roselynn and Lewis, Kathryn Ellen
Growing up on the banks of the mighty tittabawassee / Roselynn Ederer, Kathryn Ellen Lewis
Saginaw, Mich., Kathryn Ellen Lewis, 1960
p. cm. ill.
ISBN 0-9715848-8-5
1. Local History / Genealogy–United States.

Project Coordination by Bookability, Inc.

01 9 8 ◆ 6 5 4 3 2 1

Printed in the United States of America

For

Virginia Olmsted Cutler

In Celebration of Her
Half Century of Birthdays

Virginia on her 92nd Birthday
December 1, 2004

Introduction

It all started one day when Jean Grey was reading Kittie's little notebook of her childhood escapades. And being a history buff herself, Jean exclaimed, "These stories are so great—so interesting, so historical, so educational—they should be published and shared with others." Jean had been a long-time, close friend of the Olmsted Family—Gertie and especially her daughters—Virginia, Louise, and Helen. She often accompanied them when they visited Kittie at her homestead in Freeland. So as Jean read through Kittie's little notebook, she could envision Kittie's personality and humor coming alive on every page.

It was Kittie's beloved niece, Virginia Olmsted Cutler, who always enjoyed listening to the tales her Auntie and mother, Gertie, reminisced every time they were together. Although Virginia's career was as a physical education instructor, she always remained a history buff. She encouraged "Auntie" to write down those many tales she always told.

Kittie retired from her 48-year career as a kindergarten-first grade teacher in the Freeland Schools in 1959. She then spent her days writing her childhood adventures. First, she wrote them in longhand. Then she typed page after page on her old black manual typewriter. Her little notebook was 5" x 7", and her pages were typed on both sides. She also included some line drawings to illustrate her points. Finally, the book was ready for Virginia's 50th birthday in 1962. Kittie typed out three little identical 5" x 7" notebooks for her three nieces—Virginia, Louise, and Helen.

Upon reading Kittie's little notebook, I also was impressed with the Freeland history she writes about. Kittie's grandparents were some of Freeland's first generation settlers. Her grandfather, Jacob Lewis, was Freeland's first schoolteacher and first Congregational minister. Her ancestors were part of Loretto's settlers, and they helped to build the embryo community, which became Freeland. Kittie's adventures give today's readers a closer look of what life in the 1890s was really like without electricity, indoor plumbing, automobiles, tractors, trucks, telephones, washing machines, refrigerators, carpets, bathtubs, lawnmowers, radios, paved roads, and many other conveniences. Told from a child's viewpoint, Kittie's adventures tell what children a century or more ago did to play, amuse themselves, and fill their days without today's television, Nintendo's, videos, cell phones, iPods, and computers.

I am grateful for the assistance and information provided by Jean Grey, Howard Vasold, Virginia Cutler, Karen Heilborn, and Mary Lou Ederer. All the photographs used have come from my own collection or have been furnished by the following: Howard Vasold, Freeland United Methodist Church, Eddy Historical Collection of Hoyt Library, Michael and Barbara Slasinski, Morley Companies, Ralph Roberts and Dale Greve. The Olmsted Family has furnished all the Allen/Lewis/Olmsted Family photographs.

Kittie had endeared herself to hundreds of Freeland children over the years. Freeland's early history is a colorful, important part of Saginaw County's interesting history. So much of Freeland's early history is unknown to many today. So, on behalf of Kittie and myself, we sincerely wish that you will enjoy reading this book and learning about Freeland's fascinating past.

Roselynn Ederer

Table of Contents

The Treaty of 1819 is forever commemorated on the walls of the Saginaw Water Works where William Von Schipmannin painted the mural in 1976. General Lewis Cass, his aides, and Indian chiefs are signing the Treaty in the Council House while the squaws and children sit silently nearby witnessing this historic event. The Saginaw River, an Indian home, and a settler's log cabin complete the scene. Ederer Collection

The Chippewa Indians lived along the many rivers and streams in the Saginaw Valley. The primeval forest provided bountiful hunting and the rivers offered easy transportation and continual fishing. Slasinski Collection

Freeland's Early History

For centuries the Sauk Indians had roamed the Michigan Territory until the Algonquin nations—the Ottawas, Chippewas, and Ojibwas—arrived from the East and inhabited the land. The dense forest wilderness provided bountiful hunting and the many lakes and rivers offered easy transportation and continual fishing. But their traditional culture began to change in 1819. Almost 4,000 Native American Indians—men, women, and children—representing every tribe in the Saginaw Valley had assembled around the Council House on the banks of the Saginaw River. The Council House stood on a high knoll, with the thickly interlaced tree boughs forming the roof over the roughly hewed spacious platform where the Commissioner and his aides sat on rustic benches. The Indian chiefs and warriors sat around them on huge logs while the squaws, children, and young braves gathered in timid groups nearby and watched silently from the Council House's open sides. The charismatic Ogemawkeketo became the group's chief spokesman. His tribe lived at the forks of the Tittabawassee (land later owned by William Hackett).

Lewis Cass and 114 Indians signed the Treaty of Saginaw on September 24, 1819, surrendering the Chippewa's hunting grounds, their heritage of the forest, lakes, rivers, and their forefathers' burial places along with agreeing to relocate west of the Mississippi River. They permanently ceded their land stretching from Alpena to the north, Huron County to the east, and Calhoun and Jackson Counties to the south. All of present-day Saginaw, Gratiot, and Midland Counties were included in this Saginaw River district with its many tributaries. Several Indian reservations were established including one tract of 6,000 acres at the Little Forks on the Tetabawasink River (now Midland) and one tract of 6,000 acres at the Black Bird's Town on the Tetabawasink River (now Freeland). In return the United States Government would pay the Chippewa nation $1,000 in silver yearly and provide the means for them to learn agriculture. The Second Treaty signed in Detroit on January 14, 1837 ceded all these established Indian reservations to the United States Government.

John Thomson purchased 91.43 acres in section 34 in 1834. He settled there with his wife Margaret and ten children. After her death in 1860, he married Jane Reid Walker. Shown in this 1879 photo at their home at 5825 Midland Road are son-in-law William D. Cole, who married daughter Eliza, by the horse, John Thomson by the buggy, wife Jane Thomson, and two daughters. This Greek revival home was a pre-Civil War house built by a ravine that flowed to the Tittabawassee River. It was Freeland's oldest house until it was just recently torn down. Vasold Collection

Michigan became a state on January 26, 1837. A Treaty signed in Saginaw on January 23, 1838 allowed these Indian reservation lands to be sold for $5 per acre for five years, then at $2.50 per acre for two years, but no less than 75 cents per acre thereafter.

The Reservation's Red Bird Village was established west of the Tittabawassee River beginning north from the present day Tittabawassee Road. The Black Bird Village on the Reservation was established north of Red Bird Village extending along the present day North River Road. Representatives of these two villages also met annually at the Council House to receive their share of silver from the United States Government. The American Fur Company was founded in 1824 on the Saginaw River and traded furs with the Chippewas. Gardner D. and Ephraim A. Williams purchased the company in 1828 and also operated a trading post branch at the forks of the Tittabawassee. Ephraim established a

Farm Res. of PETER M^c GREGOR Sec. 27, Tittabawassee Tp. Saginaw Co. Mich.
SETTLED HERE IN 1843.

Both John and Peter McGregor purchased their farms in section 27 next to the Tittabawassee River in the 1830s. Both men leased their river fronts for 25 cents per rod to the Boom Company. The company leased miles of river front lands for their river booms and piles to help channel and control the many logs being sent down the river. Spring floods and log jams often floated logs onto farm fields next to the river. Drawing from 1877 Atlas. Vasold Collection

rapport with Wahbemanito from Red Bird Village. Ogemawkeketo eventually became the chief spokesman for the Saginaw District Chippewa nation. Both Indian villages engaged in many picturesque feasts and celebrations, singing and beating their drums at their campfires, and traveling down the river in their canoes. They lived together peacefully and shared their wild game with the white settlers, and soon began adopting the white man's manner of living.

Saginaw County was first organized on September 10, 1822 when the present counties of Saginaw, Lapeer, Sanilac, and Shiawassee were attached to Oakland County, which was organized in 1819. A tax was levied soon after. Saginaw City was also platted. On April 4, 1831 Saginaw Township, encompassing the entire present day Saginaw County, was organized. Overseers for the three districts—David Stanard for Saginaw, Eleazer Jewett for Green Point, and Charles McLean for Tittabawassee—were appointed. It also allowed for 32 total townships embracing portions of Gladwin, Midland, and Tuscola

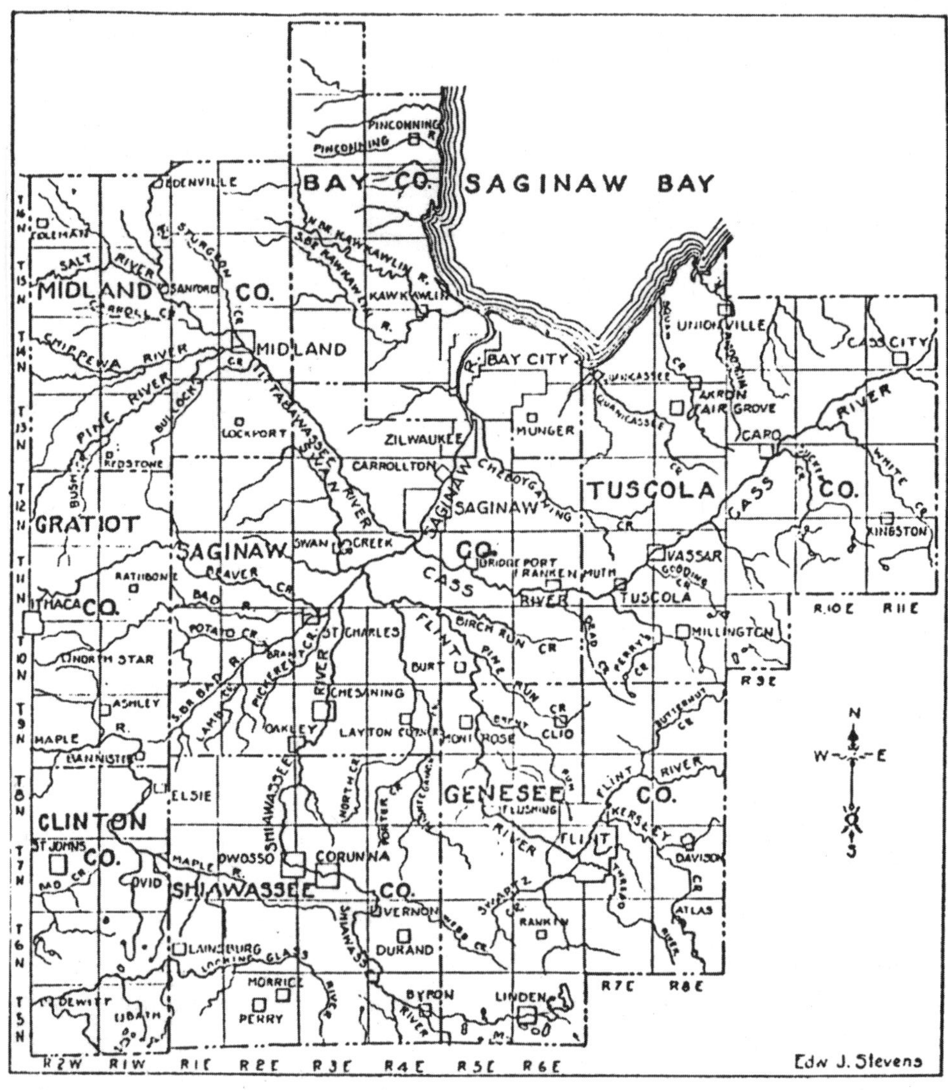

MAP 1. Waterways of the Saginaw District, Michigan

This map of the Waterways of the Saginaw River District shows the many tributaries of the Tittabawassee, Bad, Shiawassee, Flint, and Cass Rivers where they join at Green Point to form the Saginaw River. The Saginaw River is only 22 miles long, but its many tributaries total 512 miles and drain 6,250 square miles, making it a major Michigan river.
Eddy Historical Collection

Men from the Tittabawassee Boom Company are sorting logs into their owners' respective booms. Logs were marked with each owner's log mark at the lumber camp before they were floated down the rivers. The company's largest boom was located where present-day State Road Bridge crosses the river. When an owner needed logs for his sawmill, the Boom Company would tow a raft of his logs downstream to his mill. Slasinski Collection

Counties. Saginaw County's boundaries were again redrawn when it was formally organized on January 28, 1835.

Joseph Busby arrived in Saginaw City in 1833, and soon purchased land in section 23 of today's Tittabawassee Township. Although he may have been the first landowner, it is uncertain if he ever resided there. There were at least 76 parcels of land, mainly east of the river, sold in the 1830s and 1840s. These buyers came from the East, Canada, England, Ireland, and Scotland, and several of them settled there, helping to organize the township. Some of these 1830s landowners were Dr. Luke Wellington, Obadiah Crane, John McGregor, Bernard Hackett, John Thomson, Daniel Fitzhugh, Jefferson Jaquith, and Peter Cowdrey. Several others may merely have been investors or left when life in the wilderness proved too difficult.

The Goodridge Brothers took this photograph at Bryant's Trip along North River Road in the spring of 1873. Logs were floated down all the tributary rivers and streams into the Tittabawassee to be contained at the company's booms in Thomastown Township. The logs that year created an unusual log jam extending from the present-day Gratiot Road Bridge to 130 miles upstream. The entire river was jammed with logs, some two to five logs deep. Slasinski Collection

The first town meeting was held on April 5, 1841 in Obadiah Crane's rough-hewn log cabin near the Hackett property to organize Tittabawassee Township. The township was named after the river. Andrew Ure was elected Supervisor. Other local residents—Luke Wellington, Jefferson Jaquith, John McGregor, Murdock Fraser, Thomas McCarty, William R. Hubbard, Phineas D. Braley, John Benson, and Obadiah Crane—were all elected to several local offices.

Gardner D. and Ephraim A. Williams built Saginaw Valley's first sawmill near Mackinaw Street on the Saginaw River in 1834. Logs were brought from streams on the Tittabawassee River, cut into planks, and used for the local residents' building needs. Their mill was later enlarged and rebuilt after disastrous fires in 1850, 1854, and 1874. Norman Little built another sawmill

Upon arriving in 1850, William Roeser purchased considerable acreage in section 15 in Tittabawassee Township and married Therese Vasold in 1851. After platting out the Village, he was known as the Father of Freeland. He opened the first general store in 1855, became postmaster, and later opened a farm implement store in Saginaw City. His eight children have gathered outside his home upon his death on May 25, 1898. They are holding flowers and shotguns, presumably to give their father a final gun salute. Back row, from left to right: Herman, Clara, Oscar, and Albert. Front row: William, Charles, Frances, and Fred. Vasold Collection

near the present day City Hall in East Saginaw in 1836. Curtis Emerson came to East Saginaw in 1846, rebuilt this abandoned sawmill, and shipped the first cargo of clear cork pine to Albany, New York in 1847. The Saginaw Valley's excellent lumber was in demand. Saginaw's lumber industry was born! New Yorker Jesse Hoyt arrived in East Saginaw in 1849, purchased about 3,000 acres, built the pine plank Genesee Road to Flint, and began developing East Saginaw's wilderness into a town with a hotel, sawmill, lodge hall, bank, gristmill, academy, and railroad.

This Freeland Memorial Park Building was built on the same site as William Roeser's house and general store had been. The site has been named a Michigan Historic Site. Supplies for his store were brought by boat to the dock behind this building.
Ederer Collection

Eastern investors came in droves, seeking their fortunes in the newly discovered timber in northern Michigan. They purchased 40 to 80 acre tracts having good stands of pine and easy accessibility to rivers and streams for $1.25 per acre from the United States Government. A lumber camp would be built on this tract, and shanty boys would be hired to work from November through March cutting down the trees, sawing them into manageable logs, and then banking the logs on riverbanks until the spring thaw. The camp owner also built his sawmill on the Saginaw River. From April through November his banked logs would be floated down the rivers to the Tittabawassee River and to his sawmill to be sawed into lumber, transported by sailing vessels, and sold in the East.

Mammy Freeland kept this hostelry and tavern on the riverbank near Roeser's General Store. It was located on the southwest corner of Main & Washington Streets where the Freeland Bridge crosses the river. Lumbermen and river men frequently stopped at this tavern on their river journey, and they called it "Freeland's." The F&PM Railroad called it "Freelands Station." Eventually the Village was called Freeland. Vasold Collection

Although the Saginaw River is only 22 miles long, it is a major Michigan river, totaling 512 miles with its many tributaries and drains 6,250 square miles in the Saginaw River District. The Saginaw River originates where the Tittabawassee and Shiawassee Rivers join at Green Point in South Saginaw. The Tittabawassee originates in Ogemaw County and has the Tobacco, Salt, Chippewa, and Pine Rivers draining into its western banks. The Shiawassee originates in Livingston and Genesee Counties and has the Bad, Flint, and Cass Rivers as its chief tributaries.

Charles Merrill & Co. operated his Merrill Boom where present day Center Road Bridge crosses the Tittabawassee River from 1856 to 1864. He boomed more than 1.7 billion feet of logs to the Saginaw River sawmills, but his small boom became inefficient.

Mr. and Mrs. Freeland were both born in New Jersey. After arriving in Tittabawassee Township, they purchased acreage and built their tavern on the riverbank. Garrett was born in 1794 and died in 1872 in Freeland. Elizabeth was born in 1798 and died in 1871 in Freeland. She was known as Betsey and Mammy. Lumbermen always referred to the tavern as Mammy Freeland's. The Village eventually became Freeland. Vasold Collection

The Tittabawassee Boom Co. was incorporated on February 4, 1864 for 30 years. Its largest booms were located where present-day State Road Bridge crosses the river. The company also maintained boarding houses at its booms at Fitzhugh in Midland, State Road Bridge (M-46 today), and Green Point. Dams were built on the Salt, Chippewa, and Tittabawassee Rivers above Midland to control flooding so that logs could be moved as needed in the summer. The company maintained several miles of river booms and leased river front lands for their piles. John and Peter McGregor both leased their river fronts for 25 cents per rod. When the logs crowded out of the river channel and flooded the river flats, the company also paid the farmers for crop damage. In 1869 Margaret Hall was paid $50 for her garden damage and Nelson Munger $500 for his 29 acres of corn and grassland losses. Many logs often laid on farms until they were put back into the river.

Saginaw's lumber industry brought many new arrivals to Tittabawassee Township. The German Revolution of 1848 and the Great Potato Famine brought many German immigrants seeking an escape from their homeland's political, religious, and economic upheavals. In the 1850s there were 114 land parcels sold and 32 parcels sold in the 1860s. The United States Government was now

The first wooden Freeland Bridge was built in 1870 for $5,000 with the Tittabawassee Boom Co.'s help. That bridge was replaced with a steel bridge in 1895 for $10,000. The second Freeland Bridge is shown in this 1911 photo. The building on the right is the gristmill, which was built behind Roeser's Store. This made it more convenient for local farmers to get their grain ground here instead of at Saginaw City or Shattuckville. Vasold Collection

selling the Indian Reservation land on the west side of the river. Many German immigrants were establishing new farms. August M. C. and J. Ernestina Vasold and their seven children—Therese, Heinrich, August, Herman, Hugo, Clara, and Otto—arrived in 1850 and purchased 164 acres in section 28 west of the river on the Indian Reserve. Until their log house was built, they lived in a tent and used the river water. Mrs. Vasold was often ill with the ague. August Jr. served as township supervisor in 1871 and justice of the peace in 1863, 1867, and 1874. Their descendants continue to own some of the same Vasold property today.

Several members of the Munger Family came in the 1850s, also purchasing many acres of land on the Indian Reserve. Charles bought land in 1851 and

Samuel Shattuck built a sawmill and gristmill in Saginaw Township in 1842. A millpond and dam on Shattuck Creek supplied the waterpower. Farmers from Thomastown, Tittabawassee, and Saginaw Townships brought their grain to be milled and traded at the store. This mill stood where Shattuck and Midland Roads intersect today. Vasold Collection

1854 next to the river. The first Munger School was built on his property. James came in 1856 and John came in 1858. James A. Munger was a physician and merchant at Freelands Station. James A. Munger was active in township governance, serving as supervisor in 1861 and 1866 and justice of the peace in 1856 and 1879. Several of their descendants continue to reside in Tittabawassee Township today.

The three Roeser brothers—Gustav, Otto, and William—all came to Tittabawassee Township in 1850, settling east of the river. Gustav, the farmer, married Louisa Gieseke in April 1850, and they purchased 110 acres. Gustav farmed his entire life. The Freeland Community Learning Center and the Roeser Subdivision are located on his original 110-acre farm today. Otto was an attorney and served the township as clerk in 1856 and justice of the peace

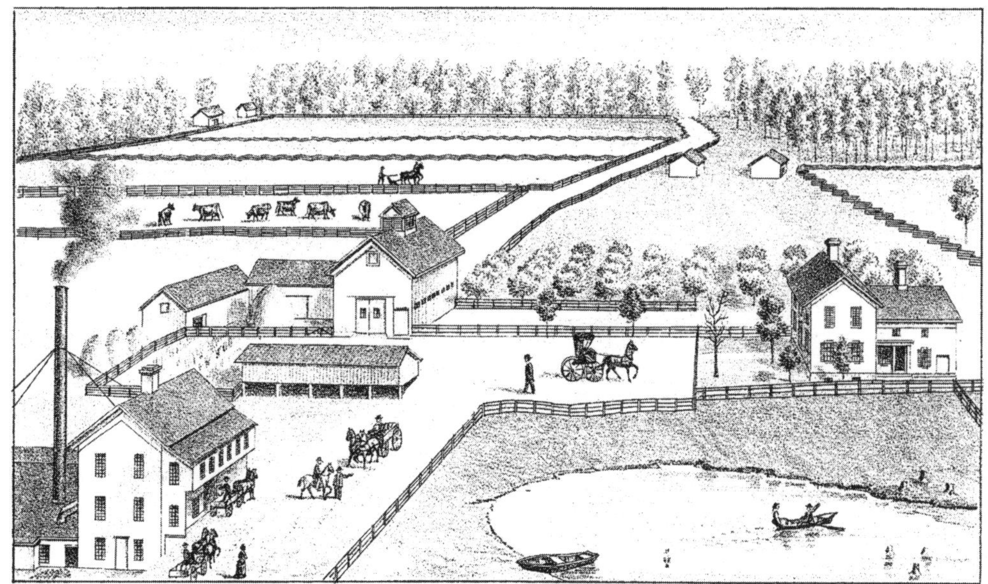

MILLS & RES. OF S. SHATTUCK
SEC. 12 SAGINAW TWP. SAGINAW CO. MICH.

This drawing is from the 1877 Atlas and shows the large community that developed at Shattuck's mill. Shattuckville emerged with several farms, five streets, a creek bridge, wagon shop, cider mill, blacksmith, general store, and post office. The Shattuck home is seen on the right side. St. John's Episcopal priests often came from Saginaw City and held services in this Shattuck home and then crossed the river to hold services at the Geddes Schoolhouse in Thomastown Township. Vasold Collection

in 1855 and 1860. He eventually went to Saginaw City and held the offices of Probate Judge, Deputy Register of Deeds, Justice of the Peace, and Board of Education. The Hill School at Cass & Bond Streets was renamed the Otto Roeser School. When this school was closed and demolished in 1950, the vacant block was renamed the Otto Roeser Park.

William Roeser was a merchant. He married Therese Vasold in 1851. He purchased considerable acreage, began farming, and then opened a general store in 1855. After he platted out the Village, he became known as the Father of Freeland. He served as postmaster when the Post Office moved to his store in 1867, township supervisor from 1873 to 1880, clerk 1858 to 1869, and justice of the peace in 1864, 1868, 1872, 1876, and 1880. When his store burned in 1886, William moved his business to Michigan & Gratiot Avenues in Saginaw City. The Wm. Roeser & Sons business carried a complete line of buggies, carriages,

The Seabird, a side wheel steamer, carried passengers and cargo along the navigable tributaries on the Saginaw and Tittabawassee Rivers in the 1880s. Starting in Saginaw City, it made frequent stops on the Bad River in St. Charles, at Shields in Thomastown, and at Freeland before continuing upstream to Midland. Transportation was easier by river than by land. Greve and Roberts Collections

harness, farm implements, farm supplies and seeds and sold their merchandise nationwide. His son Charles L. continued the business until 1904.

Europe's Great Potato Famine also brought new settlers from the United Kingdom and the East during the 1850s. Some new land buyers included Jacob H. Lewis, Ethan G. Allen, William Hilton, William Seyffardt, Peter Andre, James Frazer, George Bullock, and William Freeland. Several purchased lots around present day Midland and Pierce Roads. The small community of Loretto was platted about 1859. It was a short distance southeast of the geographical center of the township. Jefferson Jacquith started a post office in his house/store and called it Jay's Post Office. William Hilton operated a hotel, and there was a blacksmith. A daily stagecoach traveled from Saginaw City to Midland and changed horses at Loretto.

In another cluster of backwoods houses near present day Washington Street lived George Truesdale and some of his friends. They called their village

The steamer Belle Seymour, 85' long with a 27' beam, was built in Cleveland for the Muskegon River, but was used instead on the Tittabawassee beginning in August 1859. It made regular trips loaded with supplies for Roeser's Store and for lumber camps, stopping in Freeland before continuing to Midland. When the F&PM Railroad began bringing supplies in 1867, the Belle Seymour's trips were discontinued. The steamer was abandoned on the Ball flats in Midland. It later was converted to a pile driver and used for bridge and pile construction on the Tittabawassee. Photo taken in early 1900s.
Greve and Roberts Collections

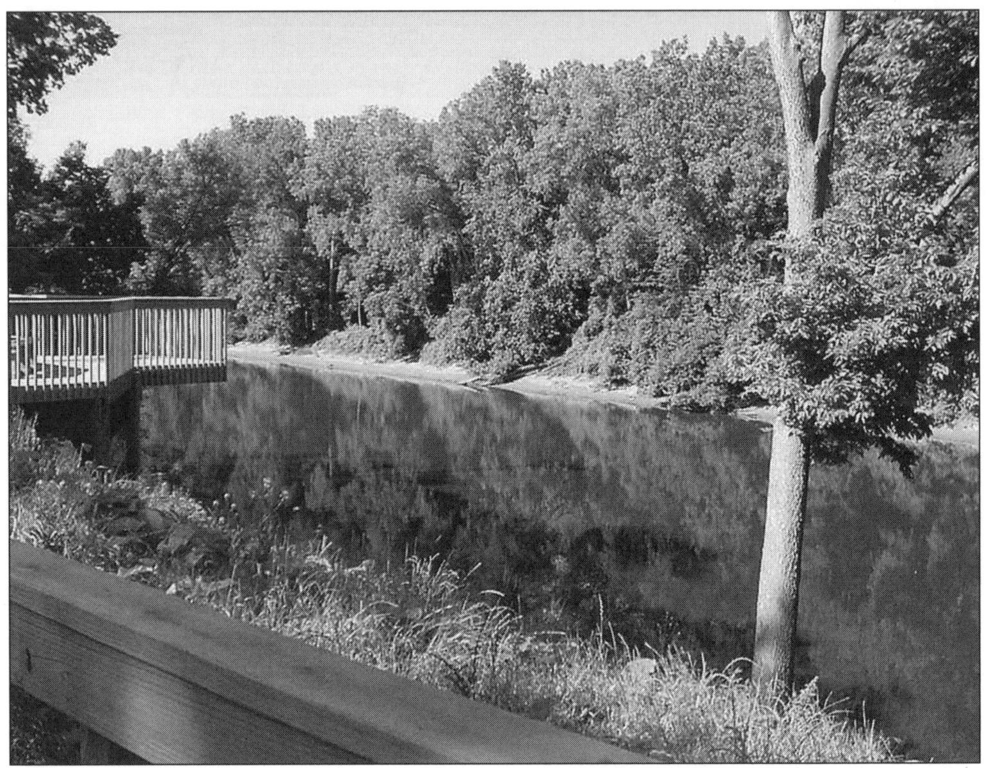

This is a present-day view of the same river dock where the Seabird and Belle Seymour made their regular stops to deliver passengers and supplies. It is located behind the Freeland Memorial Park Building. Ederer Collection

Tittabawassee. Through a shady political deal, they worked to move Jay's Post Office to their village in 1867. However, the Post Office was moved to Roeser's Store and still remained Jay's Post Office. Mammy Freeland kept a tavern on the riverbank near Roeser's Store. Lumbermen and river men often stopped at her tavern on their way along the Tittabawassee River. They always called the stopover "Freeland's" on their river journey.

The Flint & Pere Marquette Railroad Company was organized in East Saginaw on January 21, 1857. When the northern logging industry required transportation by rail, the railroad laid new roads from East Saginaw to Freeland, Midland, Averill, Clare, and Bay City beginning in 1867. The railroad then passed closer to the Tittabawassee Village instead of Loretto, so Loretto soon faded away. The train station became known as Freelands Station. The village

This Bond Sawmill was located in section 7 east of the Tittabawassee River and on the F&PM RR tracks. Other than farming, this sawmill was Freeland's only industry. Timber was harvested locally and then processed with horse teams and steam-powered equipment instead of being sent down the river to the Saginaw River sawmills. The lumber would be used in Freeland or sold to nearby communities for building houses, barns, and pine plank roads and sidewalks. These two photos were taken in the late 1880s. Vasold Collection

eventually took on the name of Freeland. The Post Office then changed its official name to Freeland also. The village has been known as Freeland ever since.

The river separated both Freelands. Freeland east of the Tittabawassee River had houses, farms, hotels, and businesses. The Indian Reservation west of the river now was laid out with many thriving farms. The Kapitan Brothers operated a rope scow ferry where present day Tittabawassee Bridge crosses the river until 1909. Orrie Crampton also operated a river ferry at Pierce Road for a short time. It was very difficult to cross the river when logs were being sent down the river to the Saginaw sawmills. So the Tittabawassee Boom Company helped to build bridges in Freeland and State Road (now M-46 in Shields) and cleared its logs from the river when Freeland's first bridge was built. Babcock & Macomber built the Freeland Road wooden bridge in 1870 for $5,000. The same bridge was replaced with a steel bridge in 1895 for $10,000 and a third bridge in 1976 for $800,000. The Tittabawassee Road Bridge was not built until 1909.

The pioneer farmers had to transport their grain by river and land all the way to Flint to be ground. This was an arduous trip and took several days. When Samuel Shattuck built his gristmill at Shattuckville in 1842, the farmers shortened their trips and expenses considerably. Then, when the gristmill was built just behind Roeser's Store, the local farmers could have their corn ground into flour and meal right in Freeland.

The river provided the easiest transportation into the township. Several steamer vessels, such as the *Seabird,* would bring cargo and passengers from Saginaw City to St. Charles, Shields, and Freeland on its way to Midland. The steamer *Belle Seymour* made daily trips from Saginaw to Freeland and to Midland beginning in August 1859. Supplies of flour, sugar, oatmeal, and crackers were brought in barrels and kegs to the river dock behind Roeser's Store. Today the location is the Veterans Memorial Park. The steamer continued on to Midland to deliver supplies for lumber camps along the way. The *Belle Seymour* made its daily trips to Freeland and Midland until 1867 when it was discontinued and left to deteriorate on the Ball flats near Midland.

Tittabawassee Township had 1,200 residents by 1877. It was one of Saginaw County's largest agricultural communities with over 22,000 acres owned and

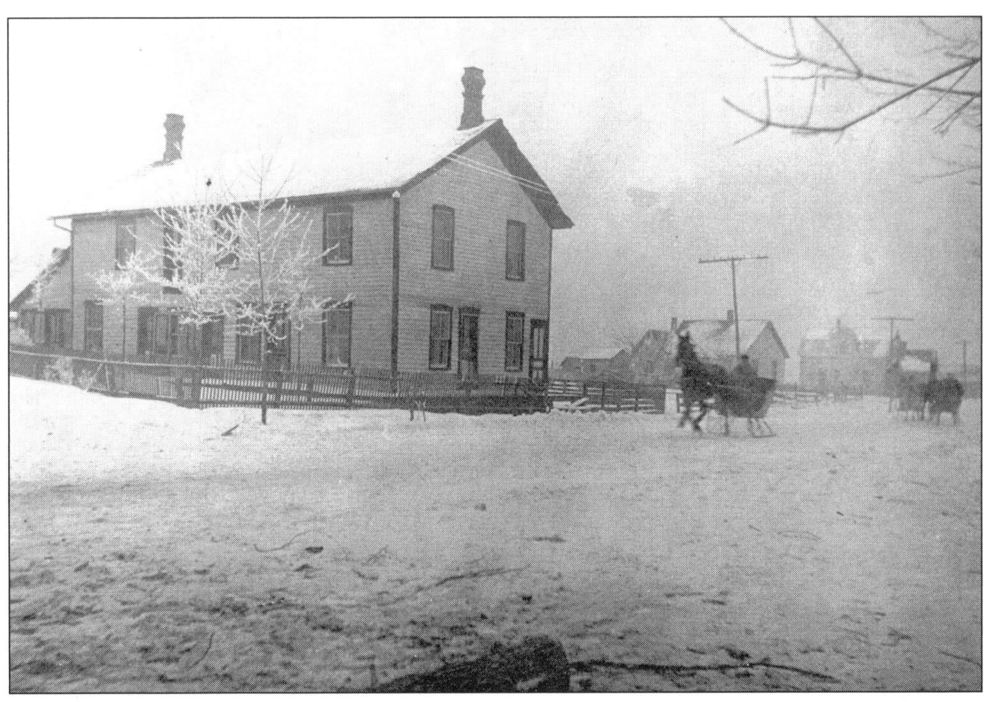

Trickey Hall was located on southeast corner of Main & Church Streets. In 1892 it served as a rooming house and provided a meeting room for the Loyal Order of Foresters. Freeland became a bustling community with the lumber industry, and several hotels were needed for the traffic passing through Freeland. Trips generally took two or three days by horse and buggy and required stopovers along the way. Vasold Collection

taxed. Wheat, corn, fruits, vegetables, horses, mules, oxen, cattle, sheep, and poultry were raised. In 1879 Tittabawassee Township had 249 farms on 8,000 improved acres. There were 1,500 people by 1880. Logging still remained an important part of the economy. Some farmers, such as John Hackett, worked on their large farms during the summer months and in their northern lumber camps, such as Averill, during the winter months using the same work crew. Other than farming, the Bond Sawmill located in section 7 east of the river on the Flint & Pere Marquette Railroad provided the only other employment.

The lumber traffic into Freeland necessitated ancillary businesses. Trickey Hall was built on Church & Main Streets and Hotel Bishop (later Rodeitcher's) was built next to Roeser's Store. The Munger, Lewis, Dietiker, and Howd's Stores were located on Main and Washington Streets. Other businesses included

The private Jaquith Cemetery is located west of Midland Road just north of Pierce Road. The cemetery is across the road from Jefferson Jaquith's property, his house, store, and post office. Several family members are buried here in this well-hidden spot surrounded by woods, just a short distance off busy Midland Road. Ederer Collection

a meat market, drug store, barber, blacksmiths, saloon, millinery, dentist, two doctors' offices, undertaker, bank, icehouse, G.A.R. Hall, feed mill, and Maccabee Hall. The village was self-sufficient.

Each township section had 640 acres, which was further subdivided into 160, 80, and 40 acres each with section 16 set aside for public schools. Joseph King built the first log school in 1854 on Noble King's donated property on Washington & Second Streets. The school census of 1881 indicated 456 children. Altogether, there were seven separate schools and districts as follows: Munger No. 1 on Gleaner Road, Porter No. 2 on Garfield Road, Freeland No. 3 on Church Street, Law No. 4 on Buck Road, Whitman No. 5 on Gleaner Road, Vasold No. 6 on Vasold Road, and Wellman No. 1 on Freeland Road. The two-story frame Freeland Schoolhouse was built on Church Street in 1872. It was

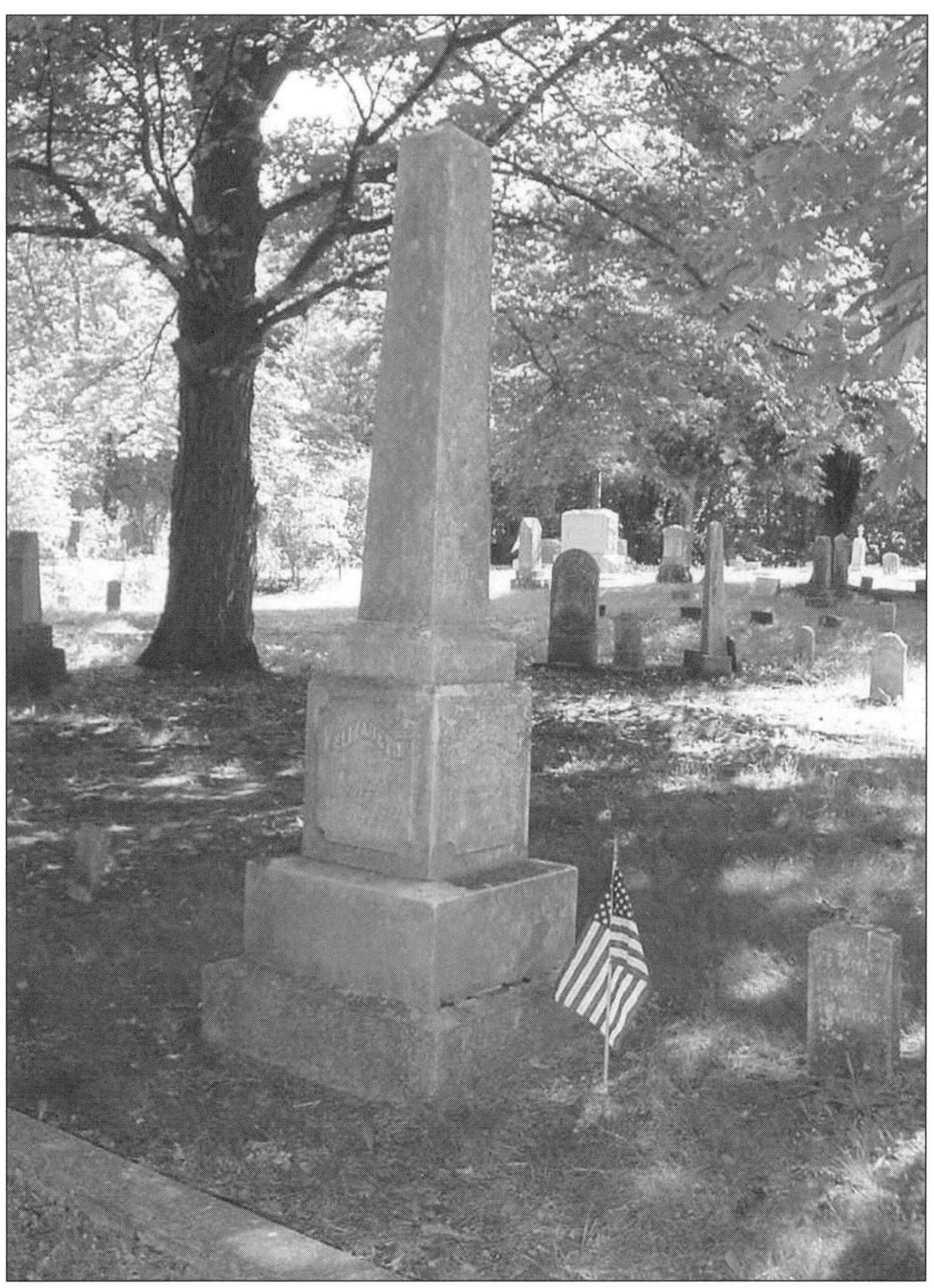

The Freeland Family graves in Pine Grove Cemetery surround this four-sided monument as follows: Garrett A. Freeland died 05/21/1872, 78 years, 8 months; Elizabeth Freeland died 12/30/1871, 73 years; William F. Freeland, born 01/04/1827 and died 05/23/1872; and Annis Freeland, born 11/24/1834 and died 10/17/1904. Ederer Collection

The hill with the log cabin on the right side is where Joseph King began his Methodist Sunday school in 1846. Pete Wilson's farm is shown on the left side. Today his farm is the Riverside Restaurant. The dirt road is the present-day M-47. This was the first Methodist Church established in Saginaw County and the third religious denomination established in the county. Freeland United Methodist Church Collection

rebuilt as a three-story brick High School, the North Building, in 1914.

The larger Pine Grove Cemetery on Midland Road accommodated burials east of the river while the smaller West Side Cemetery on North River Road was used for those who lived west of the river. It was impossible to transport a coffin across the river on a ferry, so two township cemeteries were established. Private cemeteries, such as the Vasold and Jaquith, were quite common in the 1800s and some exist yet today.

Joseph King began a Methodist Sunday school in his log cabin in 1846. He invited his neighbors to worship in his log cabin in the winter and his log barn in the summer. Circuit Rider Rufus H. Crane included the King School on his Midland Circuit, which also included Midland Bluffs, Higgins, Shields,

Guess where on the Tittabawassa, Freeland, Mich.

Girls in long dresses paddle down the Tittabawassee River in their canoes on a lazy afternoon. Michigan's lumber industry became defunct in the 1890s. Any logs still harvested were transported by rail. River traffic had declined, and the mighty river highway now became a recreational river. Residents along the river spent enjoyable afternoons fishing, swimming, canoeing, or winter ice-skating. Ederer Collection

Swan Creek, and Ure's Schoolhouse. By 1870 the 88 members could afford to pay $466.98 to the circuit rider that served Auburn, Swan Creek, and Ure's Schoolhouse. When schoolteacher Jacob Lewis became a licensed circuit rider, he and interpreter Elder Jackson preached to the Chippewa Indians across the river at Munger School.

When the Freeland Methodist Episcopal Church was organized, it was the third religious denomination and the first Methodist Church to be established in Saginaw County. In 1874 Noble King donated land at Washington & Second Streets and $1,000 for the first church building. The timber was cut from the King Estate. Lyman Macomber built this church for $3,000. The parsonage was built in 1880 and then replaced in 1910. Horse sheds were built in the back. Louis Munger rebuilt the church in 1918 for $22,000 on the same site. The third church was rebuilt on the same site in 2001.

In February 1867 Adventist M.E. Cornell began giving lectures at the

Many Native American artifacts such as these have been found along the banks of the Tittabawassee River. These tools and arrowheads are made of stone, copper, bone, and clay. These today's treasures were the Sauk and Chippewa Indians' essentials of long ago. They are part of that culture that began its decline with the Treaty of 1819. Slasinski Collection

schoolhouse. After lecturing for a month, he generated enough interest for the Seventh-Day Adventist Church to be organized. H.T. Hawley, William H. Hilton, and James A. Munger comprised the building committee. William Roeser donated the lot on the northwest corner of Second & Church Streets. Babcock & Macomber built the 40' x 60' church for $1,200. A horse shed was also built behind the church. Membership steadily grew from 37 to 50 with the greatest number being 67 total. The church was open for funerals and other occasions for Freeland residents of all denominations.

Some members of the Freeland Methodist Church began holding Sunday school in the Adventist Church and then organized the Congregational Church on February 23, 1891 with 21 members. A church that could seat 200 was built on Third Street for $2,500. Rev. Jacob H. Lewis served the church from 1892 to 1897. In 1893 membership had increased to 135. But the parsonage was not

The Bay City Grain Co. built this elevator in 1893. O.W. Mills was the superintendent. In 1899 Charles Dietiker became superintendent. Then it became the Dietiker-Howd Elevator. In 1911 it became the Freeland Elevator Company, as shown here. This elevator has served Freeland farmers for over a century. Vasold Collection

built until 1905. The Congregational and Methodist Churches often held joint evening services. The congregation disbanded sometime in the 1960s. The Township parking lot occupies the church site today.

It was always difficult for residents living west of the river to come to church east of the river. The Church of God was organized about 1890 and held services in the Munger School located on North River Road just south of Freeland Road. Usually about 25 members were present. During the winter, services were held in members' homes. The church reorganized in 1915. Their first church was built in 1948 at North River & Freeland Roads.

Catholics, Episcopalians, and Lutherans worshipped in nearby cities in Midland, Auburn, Amelith, Bay City, or Saginaw City. Episcopalian services were often held at the Shattuck home at Shattuckville. Catholics worshipped

Macadam or stone-paved roads replaced the dirt roads when more automobiles began replacing the horses and wagons. When a road was being improved, the local farmers were required to help. Martin Holubik Sr. and his neighbors used their own tractors to help build North River Road in Freeland in 1920. Vasold Collection

at Midland or Auburn until the St. Philomena Mission was organized in 1956 at the Memorial Park Building. In 1960 the church was renamed St. Agnes. Lutherans worshipped in Amelith, Bay City, or St. Matthew's Lutheran on Hospital Road. Zion Lutheran was not organized until 1931.

Traffic on the Saginaw River began declining in 1886. The railroads began transporting more lumber in and out of the Saginaw Valley in the 1870s. The logging railroad began penetrating the land previously inaccessible to the logging streams by the 1880s. The Tittabawassee Boom Co. had rafted almost 12 billion board feet of logs by its conclusion in 1894. It had rafted a larger volume than any other Michigan booming company. The new Tittabawassee River Boom Co. then operated from 1894 to 1896 and was succeeded by the Tittabawassee Boom & Raft Co. in 1897. As Michigan's forests became more depleted, there were fewer logs sent down the Tittabawassee River in the 1890s. Immense rafts of logs were now being towed from Canada to the Saginaw River. After Canada imposed a tariff, the Michigan lumber industry

This is a view of downtown Freeland along Washington Street (Freeland Road) in the early 1900s. Horse and wagons were still the general mode of transportation. Several businesses were located on this street. Vasold Collection

ceased altogether. The Saginaw River sawmills were almost entirely closed in the 1890s. The last sawmill, the Eddy Mill, ceased operating in 1900 and its equipment was dismantled and sold.

The Tittabawassee River now became a recreational river with ice skating, canoeing, swimming, and fishing activities enjoyed year round. Remnants of the booming days—piles, rafting pins, and sunken stray logs still embedded with log marks—remained in the river and were often retrieved throughout the next century. Many Indian artifacts were found along the many riverbanks and continue to be discovered yet today.

Freeland had become a thriving small agricultural community. Its three principle streets were Main (now M-47), Washington (now Freeland Road) and Church Street. The side streets south of Washington were only one block long. Depot Street was the only street north of Washington. The railroad made daily frequent trips to East Saginaw, Bay City, and Midland. It provided fast, easy transportation for Freeland residents. Agriculture was the largest industry. The Old Feed Mill was built in 1893 by the Bay City Grain Co. It was known as the Dietiker-Howd Elevator, and in 1911 became the Freeland Elevator Company.

Since then its name changed when several companies—Wolohan, Wickes, Pillsbury, and then Berger & Company—all became its subsequent owners. This rebuilt elevator has served the Freeland farmers' needs for over a century.

A fire in July 1914 destroyed many of Freeland's original store buildings on Main Street. However, the stores were rebuilt larger and better than previously. Freeland survived, and several additional new businesses have since been built.

Since the 1990s several young urban professionals have been drawn to Freeland's small town atmosphere. Farmland has given way to affluent subdivisions. Freeland has developed and prospered with a population of over 7,700 today. It serves as a crossroads for the Tri-Cities—Midland, Saginaw, and Bay City. Its MBS Airport is an international airport, serving people throughout mid-Michigan. The Saginaw Correctional Facility also houses about 1,300 inmates. The large, modern Pat's Food Center sells everything from groceries to hardware and caters to a large customer base. Modern schools now accommodate children through the twelfth grade. Plans are presently underway for a new downtown shopping complex, an expanded Memorial Park Building, and a new medical/recreational community building. And the old dirt roads—Midland and Washington Streets—now paved have become busy highways with daily heavy traffic. Modern substantial bridges carry heavy traffic over the river safely and efficiently. The Tittabawassee River is popular for its annual Walleye Fishing Festival. Freeland continues to develop as an important community in Saginaw County today. Little did those early pioneers know that their little Loretto-Tittabawassee-Freeland Village would become so large and important!

BIBLIOGRAPHY

Anderson, Harry H., *German-American Pioneers in Wisconsin and Michigan,* Milwaukee County Historical Society, Milwaukee, Wisconsin, 1971, 1989, page 368

Chapman, Chas. C. & Co., *History of Saginaw County, Michigan,* Chicago, Illinois, 1881, pages 144 – 156, 213, 289, 305 – 314, 392 – 393, 405 – 406, 445 – 458, 679 – 692, 944 – 956

Early History of Midland City, Spring of 1867

East Saginaw Courier, East Saginaw, Michigan, August 26, 1859; September 15, 1859; November 10, 1859; December 15, 1859

Ederer, Roselynn, *On The Banks of Beautiful Saugenah,* Thomastown Publishing Co., P.O. Box 6471, Saginaw, Michigan 48608-6471, 1999, pages 43 – 113, 135 – 175

Ederer, Roselynn, *Where Once The Tall Pines Stood,* Thomastown Publishing Co., P. O. Box 6471, Saginaw, Michigan 48608-6471, 2000, pages 13 – 97

Ederer, Roselynn, *Church Bells In The Valley,* Thomastown Publishing Co., P. O. Box 6471, Saginaw, Michigan 48608-6471, 2006, pages 64, 126 – 127, 156 - 161

Mills, James C., *History of Saginaw County,* Volume I, Seeman & Peters Publishers, Saginaw, Michigan, 1918, pages 12, 51 – 65, 77 – 123, 165 – 167 Volume II, pages 381 – 384

Saginaw News, January 5, 2003; September 21, 2005; September 27, 2005

Tittabawassee Township Sesquicentennial Calendar, 150 Years, 1990/1991, Tittabawassee Township Historical Society, Freeland, Michigan

Tittabawassee Township Calendar for 1993, Tittabawassee Township Historical Society, Freeland, Michigan

Tittabawassee Township Calendar for 1994, Tittabawassee Township Historical Society, Freeland, Michigan

Vasold, Howard W., *The August M.C. Vasold Family History,* pages 53 – 58, 65 – 68, 79, 81, 121, 203

Vasold, Howard W., *Research on Loretto Community, Genealogy Research,* and *General Freeland History*

KITTIE'S PATERNAL ANCESTORS

Jacob H. Lewis
Born 9/30/1827 in Dutchess County, NY
Came to Freeland 1854
Died 11/18/1923 in Freeland
3 marriages

(1)	(2)	(3)
married 12/17/1848 Mary Louise Surryhue Born 3/2/1821 Died 3/28/1864 4 children	married 6/18/1865 Aurora Jaquith born 3/19/1843 died 2/18/1893 no children	married 3/13/1895 Ella Parks born 3/7/1837 died 3/21/1910 no children

/

(1)	(2)	(3)	(4)
Mary A. Lewis b. 2/18/1853 d. 8/6/1930 married 5/1883 Herbert L. Allen b. 1/17/1857 d. 10/7/1926 1 child	William H. Lewis b. 1857 married Cora 4 children: Winnie Leon Arthur Willie	Watson A. Lewis b. 8/12/1859 d. 2/3/1944 married 3/19/1882 Katie A. Allen b. 6/11/1860 d. 1/12/1956 3 children	Florence Estell Lewis married John Symons 1 child: Earl

/ /

Louise E. Allen
b. 9/3/1890
d. 5/18/1913

(1)	(2)	(3)
Floyd Lewis b. 5/9/1883 d. 07/10/1959 married 08/23/1904 Ina Steckert b. 04/1884 4 children: Kathryn, Cleone Lella Mae, Alan	Gertrude E. Lewis b. 9/24/1888 d. 11/10/1989 married 9/16/1911 Wm. Ray Olmsted b. 7/31/1886 d. 3/6/1976 4 children	Kathryn Ellen Lewis b. 12/8/1891 d. 2/6/1985 no children "Kittie"

/

(1)	(2)	(3)	(4)
Virginia Olmsted b. 12/1/1912 E. Malcolm Cutler b. 01/06/1909 d. 06/20/1994	Helen Olmsted b. 11/5/1916 d. 05/11/2002	Louise Olmsted b. 06/23/1914 d. 01/17/2007 married 06/1940 Lawrence J. McPhee b. 03/30/1913 d. 03/20/1963 2 children	Sherman Olmsted b.08/06 /1918 d. 04/03/1997 married 02/14/1945 Elizabeth Bertrand b. 08/24/1920 d. 04/11/2004 4 children

KITTIE'S MATERNAL ANCESTORS

Ethan G. Allen III
Born 5/30/1813 in Harmony, NY
Came to Freeland after 1857
Died 6/2/1902 in Freeland
2 marriages

(1)
atherine Mary Hubbard
orn 12/24/1819
ied 2/6/1865
children
/

(2)
Olive Tarbox
married 1867 in Wisconsin
1 child in Friendship, Wisconsin:
Jesse Allen born 1868, married Agnes

1)
than Guy Allen
. 3/8/1844 (NY)
. 3/9/1919
arried Josephine
Jaquith
. 3/27/1847
. 7/26/1907

(2)
Herbert L. Allen
b. 1/17/1857 (PA)
d. 10/7/1926
married 5/1883
Mary A. Lewis
b. 2/18/1853
d. 8/6/1930
1 child
/
Louise E. Allen
b. 9/3/1890
d. 5/18/1913

(3)
Katie A. Allen
b. 6/11/1860
d. 1/12/1956
married 3/19/1882
Watson A. Lewis
b. 8/12/1859
d. 2/3/1944
3 children
/
/
/
/

(4-5-6-7-8-9)
All born in the East:
Nettie Allen (b.1842)
Ellen Allen married
John Hackett
Ephraim Allen
Pollie Ellen
Josiah Allen
John Allen -- his
(child—Hazel)

(1)
loyd Lewis
. 5/9/1883
. 07/10/1959
arried 08/23/1904
a Steckert
. 04/1884
children:
athryn,Cleone
ella Mae, Alan

(2)
Gertrude E. Lewis
b. 9/24/1888
d. 11/10/1989
married 9/16/1911
Wm. Ray Olmsted
b. 7/31/1886
d. 3/6/1976
4 children
/

(3)
Kathryn Ellen Lewis
b. 12/8/1891
d. 2/6/1985
no children
"Kittie"

)
irginia Olmsted
. 12/1/1912
. Malcolm Cutler
. 01/06/1909
. 06/20/1994

(2)
Helen Olmsted
b. 11/5/1916
d. 05/11/2002

(3)
Louise Olmsted
b. 06/23/1914
d. 01/17/2007
married 06/1940
Lawrence J. McPhee
b. 03/30/1913
d. 03/20/1963
2 children

(4)
Sherman Olmsted
b. 08/06 /1918
d. 04/03/1997
married 02/14/1945
Elizabeth Bertrand
b. 08/24/1920
d. 04/11/2004
4 children

GROWING UP ON THE BANKS OF THE MIGHTY TITTABAWASSEE

KITTIE'S CHILDHOOD MEMOIRS: 1891 to 1904

Written and
Illustrated with line drawings
By
Kathryn Ellen Lewis
"Kittie"

Lewis Publishing House
Freeland Michigan

Reprinted with permission in 2006
By
Virginia Olmsted Cutler
Louise Olmsted McPhee
Karen McPhee Heilborn

Edited with
Supplemental Notes Included
By
Roselynn Ederer

December 1, 1962

Dear Virginia,

Do you recall, Virginia, the day you and your mother came to see me and we got to reminiscing about the fun we had in our childhood? You showed quite a bit of interest in our childhood experiences—and this little book is the result of the interest you expressed that day.

Your mother and I are the last of our family, and I thought it might be worthwhile not only to leave to my nieces an account of our childhood fun but also to give some of the family background, customs, and traditions.

The book is so small that I had to omit many of our experiences such as: Our annual May picnic consisting of a group of girls ranging in age from 8 or 9 to 12; our summer job of taking the cows to the pasture through the woods in the morning and to the river at night for their drink—and our fun and imaginations along the way; our excitement and enjoyment when grain threshers arrived with their steam engine and separator for the annual threshing of wheat and oats and the big feed the women in the neighborhood put on; playing Swiss Family Robinson (a story Mother liked so well) on some piles or pilings (big posts submerged or sometimes slightly above the water of the Tittabawassee River) forming our "island"; our school box socials when we packed a supper in a crepe paper trimmed box and the auctioneer tried to get as high bids as possible. One time I told Alfred Wyman (at his request) how my box would be trimmed, so when it was "offered to the public" he began to bid and when it got up to 45 cents his eyes, with a glassy look, were popping out of his head for fear he'd lose out as he had only 50 cents. Floyd and Albert had bid all the boxes up in order to raise more money for the school. But when Albert bid 45 cents, Floyd told him to stop and let that kid have the box. You see, Floyd knew that I wanted Alfred to get it. Poor me! Most of my loves came so early in life! Too early or too late!

Then, too, the trips to the woods in spring for violets, buttercups, jack-in-the-pulpits, trilliums, hepaticas, mayflowers, phlox, and adder tongues. One time we got so warm and thirsty, we got down on our stomachs and sucked up some water from a shallow pond—trying to drink without getting any tadpoles or that green algae. To this day I can taste that stagnant water. Luckily, we escaped typhoid fever! Nutting trips to the woods on those crisp October days, lugging home heaps of hickory nuts for cakes, candy, etc. in the winter.

Then there were the hog butchering days, and the nights when Father cut the meat into roasts, hams, spareribs, side pork, steaks, etc., putting a lot of it in salt brine in ten gallon crocks and hanging hams in Grandpa's smoke house. The most fun though was the nights he made sausage and put it through a sausage machine similar to a big food grinder—the sausage coming out in long rolls. Some was packed into crocks and some into long bags (like the legs of stockings), which Mother made from unbleached factory cloth. These were hung up to freeze and then the sausage was cut into slices and fried to be eaten with buckwheat pancakes. Lickin' good! Father always shared some good cuts of meat with Uncle Guy and Uncle Herbert.

Mother was always cooking and baking and usually had a kid at each elbow waiting for a taste and a chance to "lick out the dish." Mincemeat, dried applesauce, dried corn, hulled corn, canned fruits, pickles, and everything else, which had to be sampled by two hungry girls. When peeling potatoes or rutabagas, she used to scrape some and give us the raw pulp, which we liked so well.

Spring house cleaning! What a day to remember! Everything was set out in the yard. Rooms had to be empty because carpets which were tacked down had to be taken up and hung over the clothesline where the man of the house gave it the beating of its life with a carpet beater. When the dust was finally beaten out of it, it made a tent for the girls to play in. It was very dusty because the straw from the preceding year had been walked upon and jigged upon until it was just so much chaff or dust. It was so much fun to go through the empty rooms calling in a loud voice and hearing a hollow echo bounce back! When dry from a thorough scrubbing, the floor was covered with newspapers, then a good thick padding of clean straw. In came the carpet from the line and with a carpet stretcher Father stretched it as tight as a drum and tacked it down on all sides with carpet tacks. What fun to walk over the thick straw padding! By bedtime everything was in place as clean as a whistle. Clean ticks had been filled with straw and put on the bedsprings over which had been placed the aired and plumped up feather beds. It was like sleeping on a high soft cloud. Gradually after a lot of sleeping on it, it got back to normal height.

Virginia at age 50.

I could go on and on but I must not. Many hours of my first retirement year were spent in preparing this "valuable creation." I did it all in longhand first—changing it here and there as I typed. All of the incidents recorded are true but not necessarily in the right sequence. My English isn't always too correct, and the gremlins too often played hob with my spelling. I guess they got in when I wasn't looking. The pictures are not intended to be "works of art" but rather cartoons. Too often I got the thumbs on the little finger side, or the big toe confused with the little toes. You'll have to read each chapter to get the meaning of each picture.

You may think Kittie was too self-centered—writing so much about herself, but you see, this is a portrayal of life as she saw it—through the eyes of a child. Often Gertie and Murl were occupied with other interests while Louise and Kittie were playing together. Louise and Kittie were double cousins and bosom chums—nearly always together. She died when she was 22—which was an awful blow. An only child, she used to be envious of larger families and would say, "I had a brudder but he died."

This may seem an odd birthday gift. The many hours of work were involved in it. I thoroughly enjoyed doing it. And, at least, it's different. I'll bet you never had a birthday gift like it?

Please excuse all mistakes. I hope you get as much fun reading the book as I did writing it.

My very best wishes for a very happy birthday—and a half-century more of them!

With love,
Auntie

Table of Contents

CHAPTER 1

BABYHOOD

The weather-beaten house, better known as the old Haines House, stood some distance back from the road now known as U.S. 10 just one mile south of Freeland on the same side toward the river. The Haines Gully stretched along and behind the house and sloped to the flats along the Tittabawassee River. The house had three rooms on the main floor, a summer kitchen, and an attic upstairs. The entire upstairs was one big room. Downstairs on the main floor was a parlor-dining-room combination, two bedrooms, and a summer kitchen. A cellar had been dug under the house but was never finished and was not used.

In the front bedroom Katie Lewis had been in labor all evening. Mrs. Jenny Emery, who was often engaged by the local women in the capacity of midwife, was with her all night. It snowed during the night so that by Tuesday morning, December 8, 1891, the ground was white with snow. The sun shone clear and bright on this crisp, cold day. The family physician was summoned. Dr. Cubbage delivered a baby girl after Katie's long night of suffering labor pains. Mrs. Emery acted as midwife. Then Katie's sister-in-law, Mary Allen, came and stayed with her all day and night. Aunt Mary always fancied herself worse off than the patient.

Katie was in such pain that someone (probably Aunt Mary as she had a phobia for medicine) gave her some of Grandma's pain medicine. Katie later said she must have been allergic to it—it didn't stop the pain but made her delirious. However, after several days she "pulled through" without any serious complications.

Mrs. Emery's sister, Ethel, was engaged to do the work while Katie was confined. Watson and Katie Lewis were very happy to have another little girl.

Gertie, a chubby little girl of three, was delighted to have a baby sister and guarded her very carefully—almost jealously. Floyd was almost nine and not particularly interested in babies. For nearly five and one-half years until Gertie was born in 1888 he was the center of attention and the axis on which all the neighborhood relatives revolved: Uncle Guy and Aunt Josie Allen, Grandpa and Grandma Lewis, Uncle Herbert and Aunt Mary Allen—to say nothing about Father and Mother, Watson and Katie Lewis. It was quite a blow to his egotism to have to share the attention with Gertie. He rather resented it, but by the time this next baby arrived, it was not such a jolt. He was older now and really thought she was rather cute.

In due time the relatives arrived with suggestions for the baby's name. Mother had decided upon the name of "Mildred." The relatives had wanted Gertie named Catherine after their mother, our Grandma Catherine Allen. But Mother had named her Gertrude. So this baby simply must be named Catherine. Uncle Guy had no children. Aunt Ellen Hackett had one son, and Aunt Pollie Allen was single. So of course, they had a perfect right to select the name!

Finally Mother acquiesced and named her Kathryn, secretly saying "But we'll call her Kittie because she's so little. The next baby I'll name what I please." So Kittie she'll be throughout this story.

One day John Buzell, an uncle by marriage (husband of Grandpa Lewis' sister Kathryn) made a great fuss over the baby and said he was going to take her home with him. Frantic with fear Gertie literally became a miniature cyclone and tore into him with tooth and nail. She scratched and bit and kicked Great Uncle John and said he couldn't have her baby. Badly beaten, he relinquished all claim to the infant. Inwardly Mother was rather tickled that he had met his match, because she thought he had no right to tease a three-year-old that way. People hadn't studied child psychology then and some people always thought it fun to tease little children.

When Dr. Cubbage came in one day, he said to Gertie, "We've got a new little baby boy at home." "I don't care if you have," said Gertie. "I've got Kittie."

When she was six months old, Kittie had scarlet fever. She had a "gathering" which formed in her neck. Good old Dr. Cubbage lanced it and removed about a cupful of pus. Kittie had always carried the scar, very close to the jugular vein.

One day during the following fall Kittie lay very listlessly in her cradle. She neither cried nor made any fuss so Mother didn't realize she was such a sick child. Mrs. Haviland happened to come visiting and noticed that the baby paid no attention to anything. "You've got a very sick baby there," she said. "I knew one like that that died." Fear clutched at Mother's heart. Father immediately drove to Freeland for Dr. Cubbage (no phones in those days). The doctor came and pronounced it pneumonia. He had Mother make a jacket of cotton batting, and covering it with turpentine and lard, wrapped little Kittie in it. For several days she ran a high temperature, paying little attention to anything except to say, *"Water! Water!"* in a weak little voice. After her recovery, her neck was so little—only a few inches in circumference—that Father and Mother carried her about on a pillow. Apparently they didn't want her to lose her head—just yet!

At two years of age Kittie's parents had to take her to a dentist in Saginaw. A tooth grew through the side or top of the gum and was pressing against her upper lip. Kittie stood at the office window happily watching a woman pushing a baby buggy down the street. "We're ready for the little girl," said the dentist. Then Father carried Kittie to the chair, and she whooped it up. She was more frightened than hurt.

Grandpa and Grandma Lewis (Step-Grandma #1) lived just across the side road. They had taken a great fancy to Kittie because she was the baby. Grandma was dying of consumption as it was then called. She hadn't seen Kittie since her bout with pneumonia, so one day in February she asked to see her. So wrapping her up well Mother took Kittie over to their house. In a high, feeble voice Grandma kept saying "Kittie, Kittie" and smiling. That night she died,

Gertie is five years old, and Kittie is two years old in this 1893 photo.

leaving Grandpa all alone. So the family moved in with him into a much better, warmer house—but with less family privacy.

Grasping Aunt Mary (Father's older sister) wanted the carpet that covered Grandpa's living room floor. So Mother sewed and sewed carpet rags for months and had a rag carpet made to cover that large room. Life with Grandpa wasn't too pleasant for Mother, and she longed to be in a home of her own.

The next summer while walking out by the hedge fence Kittie stepped upon a thorn and got an infection in her foot. So again she needed extra attention.

Later that summer Kittie was very ill with rose fever, the doctor called it. What a worry that little bundle of life must have been to her parents in her early childhood. Mother took care of her days, and Father took over nights. Once again good nursing and the old family Doctor Cubbage brought her through. Much of Kittie's early life was spent in the old spindle cradle. But she was determined to live!

At the age of four Kittie contracted whooping cough from Floyd and Gertie. Mother didn't realize that Gertie had it as she only whooped once—and that was in a crowd at some gathering. But Kittie whooped and whooped and nearly whooped her little head off. Mother had a pail of wood ashes handy, and whenever Kittie started to whoop she'd run to that pail as fast as she could because it nearly always made her vomit.

When Kittie was four years and three months old in March 1895, Grandpa went away but didn't tell where he was going. Then the bomb exploded! He wrote Father that he had remarried and wanted him to meet him and his new wife at the train on Saturday night. Father took the light wagon so he could pick up her trunk and other baggage. The new Step-Grandma #2 (Ella Parks), a widow, looked quite a lady as she alighted from the train. Dressed in a pretty brown suit, she wore a natural color straw hat trimmed with brown and matching thin shoes and stockings. Her outfit was hardly adequate for open-air transportation

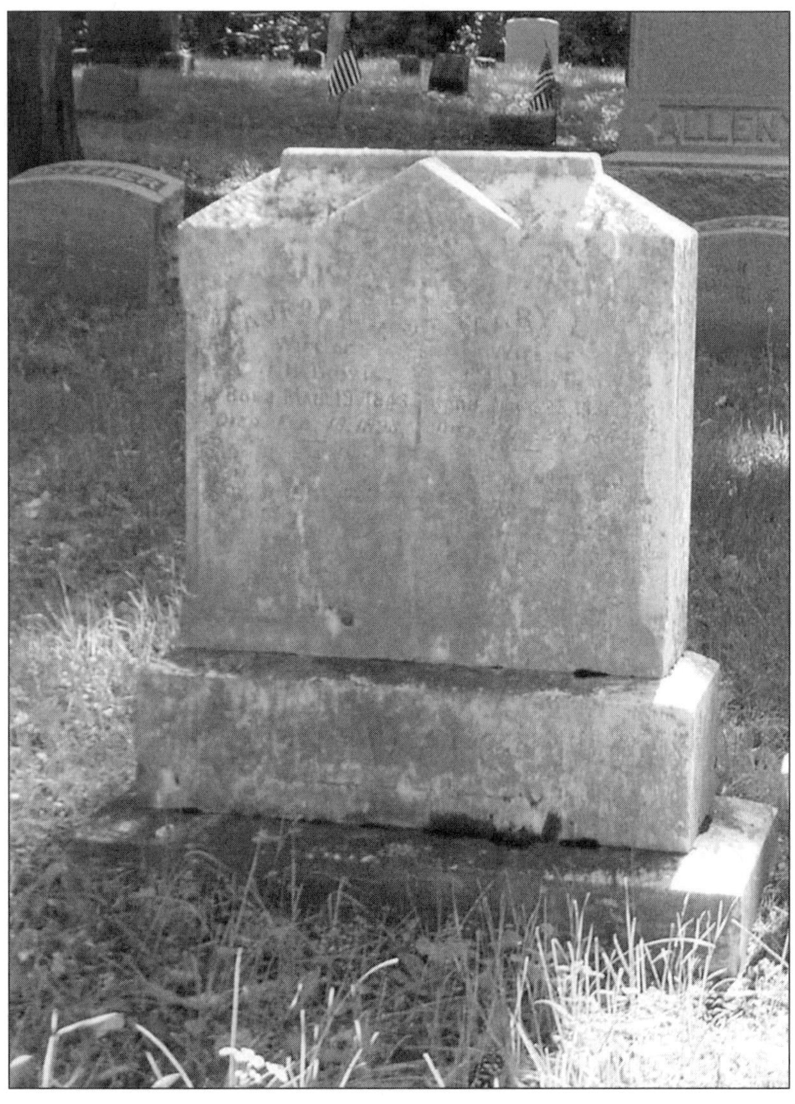

Jacob H. Lewis' first and second wives are buried side by side with this tombstone. Mary Louise Surryhue Lewis died on March 28, 1864. The second wife, Aurora Jaquith Lewis died on February 18, 1893. Ederer Collection

in this cold March weather. She developed a cold and was ill for two weeks. Grandpa and Grandma had their own apartment—a good-sized living room and bedroom in the upright. But most of the time Mother did the work and got all the meals while Grandma played lady and semi-invalid. Grandma had come from Coldwater, Michigan and was unaccustomed to farm life. Her son, Bruce, had just married so she came here and let him live in her house in Coldwater.

Floyd came home from school one day and wanted the gun. At school he had discovered that folks were going to give Grandpa a charivari. A newly married couple usually expected one when they returned from their honeymoon. People for miles around would come at night with guns, horns, cowbells, tin pans, firecrackers, and every other noisemaker. At a signal they all let loose and it sounded as though all pandemonium had let loose. Mother said at the first loud blast Floyd lost all of his bravado and said no more about the gun. After the noisy serenade it was customary for the groom to treat the crowd. Wasn't that a barbarian relic?

NOTES

Gullies were naturally eroded streams, culverts, or deep ditches that collected rain and runoff waters and drained into the Tittabawassee River. All the early pioneers settled near a gully and took their water from this stream. This water was more pure than the river water. The gully would be named after the home's inhabitant. The Haines House was across the road from Jacob H. Lewis' farm on the southeast corner of Pierce and Midland Roads. An auto wash business occupies the same site today.

All the relatives lived within the neighborhood. Jefferson Jaquith's house, store, and his Jay's Post Office were next to Jacob H. Lewis' farm on the northeast corner of Pierce and Midland Roads. His daughter, Josephine, married Guy Allen. Uncle Guy and Aunt Josie were Ethan G. Allen and Josephine Jaquith Allen. They lived next to the Jacob Lewis farm on the Jaquith farm, and their property is shown as Josephine Allen in the 1877 Atlas. Step-Grandma #1 (Aurora) was another daughter of Jefferson Jaquith.

Jacob H. Lewis' first and second wives are buried side-by-side of each other at the Pine Grove Cemetery. #1—Mary Louise Surryhue Lewis died on March 28, 1864; #2—Aurora Jaquith Lewis died on February 18, 1893. Jacob married Ella Parks on March 13, 1895. She died on March 21, 1910 and is buried next to Jacob H. Lewis.

Freeland was the cluster of homes and businesses along Main and Washington Streets. Dr. William B. Cubbage's house was on Washington Street. Taylor Undertakers occupied the same site later.

CHAPTER 2

GRANDPA AND GRANDMA LEWIS

Grandpa had been preaching for a group of Congregationalists who held services in the Adventist Church on Church Street until their church was built in 1892. Then he was hired to preach for the staggering annual sum of $200. This was a farming community and much of the salary was paid in donations.

A donation party was held at Grandpa's. Mrs. Nims brought six pullets, charging 50 cents each so she was credited with $3 toward his salary. Grandpa raised hens also, so her donation probably wasn't appreciated too much. It was a case of too many pullets in the henhouse and not enough money in the purse. Many other kinds of farm produce were donated and the donors given financial credit on the books according to the prevailing market price. Grandpa then had to take the "donation" to town to sell and turn into cash. The church members were always behind on his salary.

Before becoming a preacher Grandpa was a teacher—the first one in the Freeland School which was a log building on what is now Washington Street. Then he taught in the Law and Porter Schools. He was converted to Christianity while teaching in the Porter School. He felt called to preach so he bought commentaries, harmony of the gospels, and other Biblical helps and studied at home. He was a brilliant scholar and had a wonderful memory. He knew the Bible from A to Z and could recite passage after passage from memory. His delivery was very good—he could speak fluently. He always said he graduated from "Brush College." He performed the marriage ceremonies of practically everyone in the country and was very popular.

When Father was a young boy Grandpa became a circuit rider and was

The teachers and school children have gathered in front of the one-room Porter School at 6125 Garfield Road in this 1890s photo. Porter No. 2 was one of seven school districts in Freeland. Jacob Lewis taught at this school, which was a short distance from his farm. The old Porter School building has been converted into present-day apartments. Vasold Collection

gone several days at a time. While he was trying to get the Indians along the Bay Shore converted, his four children were home raising Cain. They had a very young stepmother (Aurora Jaquith) who was the sister of Uncle Guy Allen's wife (Josephine Jaquith). Aurora was never very strong and had lived a rather sheltered life, unaccustomed to children. She couldn't do anything with the boys so she just let them go and laughed at their many escapades. William and Watson were given free reins.

Father and Uncle Will (two years older than Father) used to put a board out the upstairs window with one boy on the inside end and the other on the outside end. This was only one of their many dangerous escapades. Uncle Will was born with a clubfoot and had to have a shoe made to order. To get his way he used to kick with that odd-shaped foot, and every one was anxious to keep

The Dan W. Smith Photographer in Saginaw City took this photograph of Jacob Lewis, probably in the 1880s.

out of its range. Step-Grandma #1 couldn't do a thing with him. Because of his handicap he always got the preference. As he grew up he was sent off to school and became a teacher. He was a brilliant mathematician and could have taught in college, but he was unstable in his ways. Father so wanted to be a bookkeeper as he, too, had a mathematical mind and loved working with books. But he had to stay home and manage the farm—something he never liked very well. On the other hand, Mother loved a farm.

Step-Grandma #2, the only one Gertie and Kittie knew, didn't care much for housework. Sometime before marrying Grandpa she had done quite a number of large oil paintings—a few of which hung in their living room. Kittie, a frequent visitor who loved to make pictures of her own, often stood looking up at those oil paintings with admiration. One was a large painting of two deer standing in a stream silhouetted against the wooded background. The stag's antlered head was held up proudly as he stood on guard for his gentle mate. Grandma said "Some day, Kittie, I want you to have some of these pictures."

In her mental eye Kittie could already envision that painting hanging in her own house with her own children admiring it as she so often did. But guess who got the pictures. Aunt Mary, of course!

Grandma had such a peculiar laugh. Instead of going "Ha, ha, ha," she always went "Hoo, hoo, hoo." Grandpa and Grandma used to take Kittie with them in the horse and buggy when she was quite young. Grandma used to say, "You always wanted the horse to run. You would look up at your Grandpa and say 'Mait Elsie Wun!'" and then she would "Hoo, hoo, hoo."

Grandma was clever at making fancy work. One day she called Gertie, Louise, and Kittie over to her house and gave each a bonnet she had made. Gertie's was of black wool worked with pink yarn with a high part at the back gathered on the rest of the bonnet. It was pretty and well made but made after an old pattern. Mother was afraid she wouldn't wear it. Louise's was brown taffeta silk lined and trimmed with red. Kittie's was the prettiest of all—pretty taupe silk taffeta lined and trimmed with pink, and a matching muff trimmed at both ends with bands of fur. Grandma probably made them out of odds and ends that she had on hand.

Three proud, happy little girls marched off for school the next morning. Mother had a feeling of misgiving over Gertie's as it was noticeable for the high

Farm Res. of J. H. LEWIS
Sec. 21, Tittabawassee Tp. Saginaw Co. Mich.

This drawing of the Jacob H. Lewis farm is taken from the 1877 Atlas. Jacob purchased 93 acres in section 21 in 1854. He owned land on both sides of Pierce Road shown on the right side. Midland Road is on the left and forefront of the drawing. The acreage in lower right, or south of Pierce Road, is where the Loretto community began. Vasold Collection

part that was puckered into the bonnet proper.

The following morning Gertie refused to wear her bonnet—the boys had shouted "Here comes old Mother Goose!" That had done it! Mother didn't do any urging because she knew that Gertie's little soul had had a humiliating experience. And she set about making Gertie a new bonnet of more contemporary design. But Kittie loved her pretty bonnet and muff—the muff especially as she always had such cold hands. Mother used to knit wristlets for her to match her mittens—as a protection from the wind and snow that were bound to make their way up one's coat sleeve.

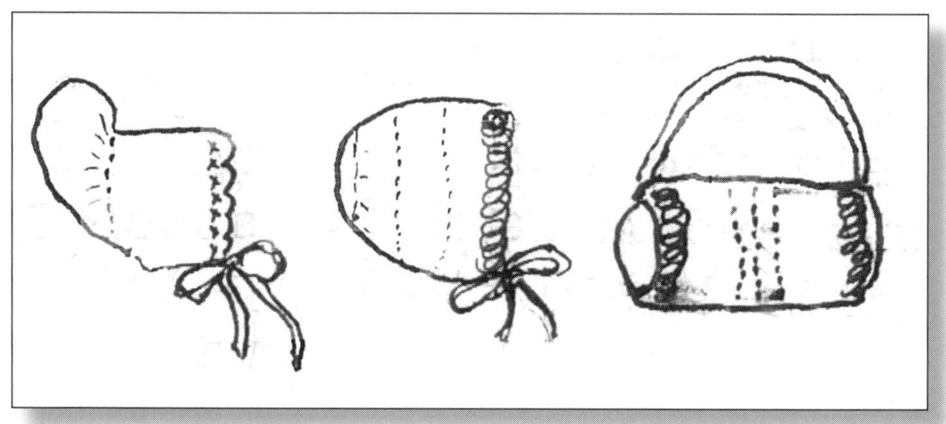

NOTES

Jacob H. Lewis migrated to Grand Blanc in 1836. He was self-taught and began teaching school at age 19 in 1846. He and his first wife, Mary Louise Surryhue Lewis, came to Tittabawassee Township in 1854. He purchased 93 acres in section 21 on November 7, 1854. His four children—Mary, William, Watson, and Florence—were born during this marriage. Mary died in 1864 and he had two subsequent marriages. He engaged in farming. He lived in the Loretto community and also ran a small store for a time.

Jacob was very active in township governance. He served as Tittabawassee Township Supervisor on six different occasions in 1856-1857, 1859-1860, 1862, 1865, 1867-1869, and 1872. He also served as Township Clerk in 1870 and 1873-1876.

Jacob taught school for 15 years until 1861. Freeland's first school was built in 1854 on the northwest corner of Washington & Second Streets. Jacob was the school's first teacher. Freeland had seven one-room school districts. Jacob also taught at the Law School at 9310 Buck Road and at the Porter School at 6125 Garfield Road.

While teaching at Porter School, he self-studied and became a preacher for the Wesleyan Methodist Episcopal Church. He then became a circuit rider for the Midland Circuit, preaching to organized classes, which also included the Freeland Methodist Episcopal Church. He also preached for the Indians from the Black Bird Indian Reservation located across the river along

This Seventh-Day Adventist Church was built on the northwest corner of Second & Church Streets in 1867 for $1,200. The congregation had only 67 members, but the church was open for funerals and other occasions to all denominations. After the Congregational Church was organized in 1891, Jacob Lewis preached to its members in this church until their own church was built on Third Street in 1892. Vasold Collection

The Lewis Family plot is located in the Lynch Block 1, lot 4 of Pine Grove Cemetery. The graves are from left to right: Herbert Allen died 10/7/1926; Louise Allen died 05/18/1913; Mary Allen died 08/06/1930; Jacob H. Lewis died 11/18/1923; Ella Lewis died 03/21/1910. Ederer Collection

present-day North River Road. Elder Jackson was part Indian and served as the interpreter for the Indians when church services were held at the Munger Schoolhouse west of the Tittabawassee River.

A Seventh Day Adventist congregation had organized in 1867 and built their church on the northwest corner of Second & Church Streets. Another group left the Methodist Episcopal Church and organized the Congregational Church in 1891 with 21 members. Jacob became their preacher and used the Adventist Church until the Congregational Church was built in 1892 on Third Street at a cost of $2,500. It could seat 200 people. By 1893 there were 135 members. The Methodist and Congregational members often shared evening services. Jacob was their only minister until 1897. A parsonage was built in 1905.

Herbert and Mary Allen's daughter, Louise Allen, lived nearby Kittie and Gertie. They grew up together and became fast friends. They were a threesome during their many childhood activities. Louise was a first cousin to the girls.

Chapter 3

The Granary House

Mother was eager to live with her young family in a house of their own. So soon after Grandpa married Step-Grandma #2 the family moved into a house just across the side road—on the very spot where the Loretto Hotel stood in the little settlement of Loretto before the Village of Freeland came into being.

In the early days Loretto was the halfway stopping place between Saginaw and Midland. It consisted of the hotel, livery stables where the stagecoach horses were changed in making the trip from Saginaw to Midland over heavy clay roads, a store, blacksmith shop, a few houses, and the Jay Post Office. It was named Jay after Jefferson Jaquith in whose home it was located. He was the postmaster, and the Post Office was simply a high-top desk with pigeonholes into which the mail was placed. This was in operation when Uncle Guy was serving in the Civil War so all his letters came there. Mr. Jaquith was the father to the Jaquith sisters mentioned previously and who married Jacob Lewis and Guy Allen.

This house into which the family moved was a granary on Grandpa's farm. They had it moved over there, and then Father changed it into a house. There they lived until they moved to Freeland in 1918. At first the house had a parlor, a dining room-kitchen combination, a pantry, and three bedrooms. Later Father built on a large kitchen and a large pantry and doubled the size of the back bedroom. Floyd slept in the back bedroom. Mother and Father slept in the middle one. And while they were small, Gertie and Kittie slept in the same room in a dark red spindle bed. The front bedroom was the guest room.

The original pantry became a hallway connecting the dining room with the new kitchen with storage space built in both ends. The entire upstairs was a big attic where the girls played on rainy days and did whatever they pleased.

It was in this house that Kittie could recall the first Christmas in her memory. As usual she was ill and couldn't go to the annual church tree and entertainment. Mother, Floyd, Gertie, and other relatives in the neighborhood went while Father stayed home with Kittie. They kept the parlor door closed until evening. And when the door was finally opened displaying a tree trimmed with lighted wax candles, fancy paper ornaments that Mother had made, and popcorn strings, Kittie's eyes grew large with the beauty and wonder of it as she "Oh'd" and "Ah'd" to Father's pleasure.

The open well at this house was the same well that stood at the back of the Loretto Hotel. All their drinking water came from that well. It had a square wall built over the middle of the curb. Instead of the moss-covered bucket made famous in the song, *The Old Oaken Bucket,* a pail was tied on the end of a long rope which had to be given the right kind of a flip just before reaching the water in order to tip it upside down and bring it up full with its cold, refreshing water—the best water in the country! In summer on hot days Mother would hang crocks of butter, pressed chicken, etc. down there to keep them cool before the days of refrigeration. She tied the crocks in heavy dishtowels and suspended them by ropes within a few feet of the water.

Gertie had difficulty in talking plainly. She had a way of adding *d-l-e* on many words and often the only way she could make herself understood was by acting out the word. One day the churn dasher broke and there was a big churning to be done. So Gertie was sent over to borrow Uncle Guy's. The only way Guy and Josie could interpret "chay-daddle" was when she pantomimed the up and down motion of churning.

Aunt Ellen Hackett was quite disgusted with her talk when she visited there one day. She said she could have heard a lot of news if she could have understood Gertie. "Ma went to a fudl up to feedle," Gertie told her. (A funeral—Freeland) It was Eddle, Poddle, and Weedle—Ellen, Pollie, and Louise—all day long, and many, many other uninterruptible expressions. Aunt Ellen said, "If Kittie had a good teacher she'd be a plain talker." But it was a strange paradox—as much as Kittie worshiped Gertie she didn't seem to copy her strange lingo.

Many happy years were spent in the old granary house. Later observations

show that it takes more than material things to make a happy family. There was a feeling of love and security and of being wanted that meant far more than temporal things. It was a home where hospitality was shared by friends and strangers alike. Father was a quiet man but loved his family and made many sacrifices for them. Mother was the jolly, friendly kind and welcomed everyone with open arms. Young and old alike were very fond of her. There was a feeling of freedom and comfort there that seemed lacking in some other homes that had more worldly goods.

Father and Mother had agreed to talk things over before making important decisions. So the children never experienced that wavering between two opinions that often gives them a feeling of insecurity. When the children wanted to do something they usually asked their mother first. If she wasn't quite sure she would say, "Go ask your father," and he would say, "Ask your mother." But if it was a real important matter and he had to say "NO", they knew it would do no good to go back and coax Mother. It was like the child in the poem:

Oh, it's hippity hop to bed,
I'd rather sit up instead;
But when Father says 'must'
There's nothing but just
Go hippity hop to bed.

Father never spanked or hurt the children in any way—he didn't have to. He had a look in his eye that said very plainly "I mean what I say so don't do any coaxing." And they didn't. He was the reserved type and didn't always show his feelings outwardly, but when any emergency arose in the family or neighborhood it was always Father who, because of his calmness and ability to think well in times of stress, arose to the situation and left his own work or pleasure to help those in need. They all valued his opinion because it was never given on the spur of the moment, but only after serious consideration.

The framed motto on the parlor wall seemed to give the right atmosphere in the home:

Bless the Lord, O my soul, and forget not all His benefits. Psalms 103:2

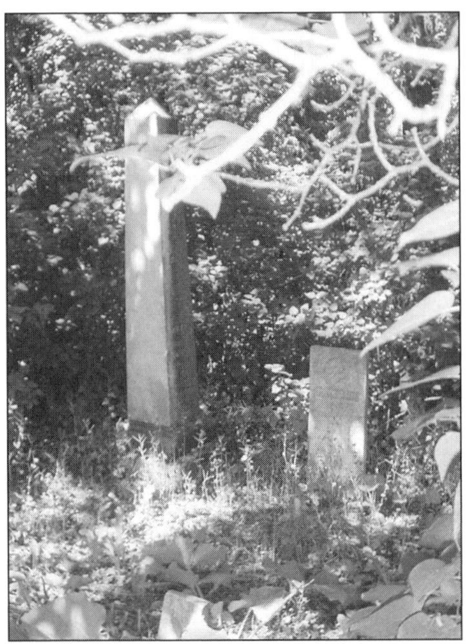

The private Jaquith Cemetery is just across Midland Road from Jefferson's Post Office in a secluded spot surrounded by woods. Several family members are buried here. The tall tombstone on the left is Jefferson Jaquith's who died in 1870. Ederer Collection

NOTES

A few log buildings were built in the late 1840s and early 1850s on present-day Midland Road (US-10 or M-47), a short distance southeast of the geographical center of the township east of the Tittabawassee River. It was named Loretto and platted by 1859. (An auto wash business occupies the same site today on the southeast corner of Pierce & Midland Roads.) A stagecoach traveled from Saginaw City to Midland on rough highways and changed horses at Loretto. Jefferson and Sarah Jaquith and their four children came in 1839. He purchased 73.21 acres in Section 21 in July 1845. Jefferson Jaquith ran a store and Post Office from his house beginning with April 23, 1856. He named it the Jay Post Office, and all mail during the Civil War passed through this Post Office. There were also the Loretto Hotel, a blacksmith shop, hostelry, Hilton Tavern, and a few houses. On June 10, 1863 it became the Village of Loretto with D.M. Burgess as Proprietor. Some of the other land owners or residents in Loretto were William Seyffardt, Luke Wellington, William H. Hilton, Peter LeRoy, Albert Purchase, Jacob H. Lewis, William Doran, Joseph Whitmore, Charles Holbrook, John Thomson, Sr., L.W. Haines, George B. Brooks, John A. McGregor, Anisette Saleno, and James Champy. Several had purchased small parcels as an investment, believing a town would emerge in this location.

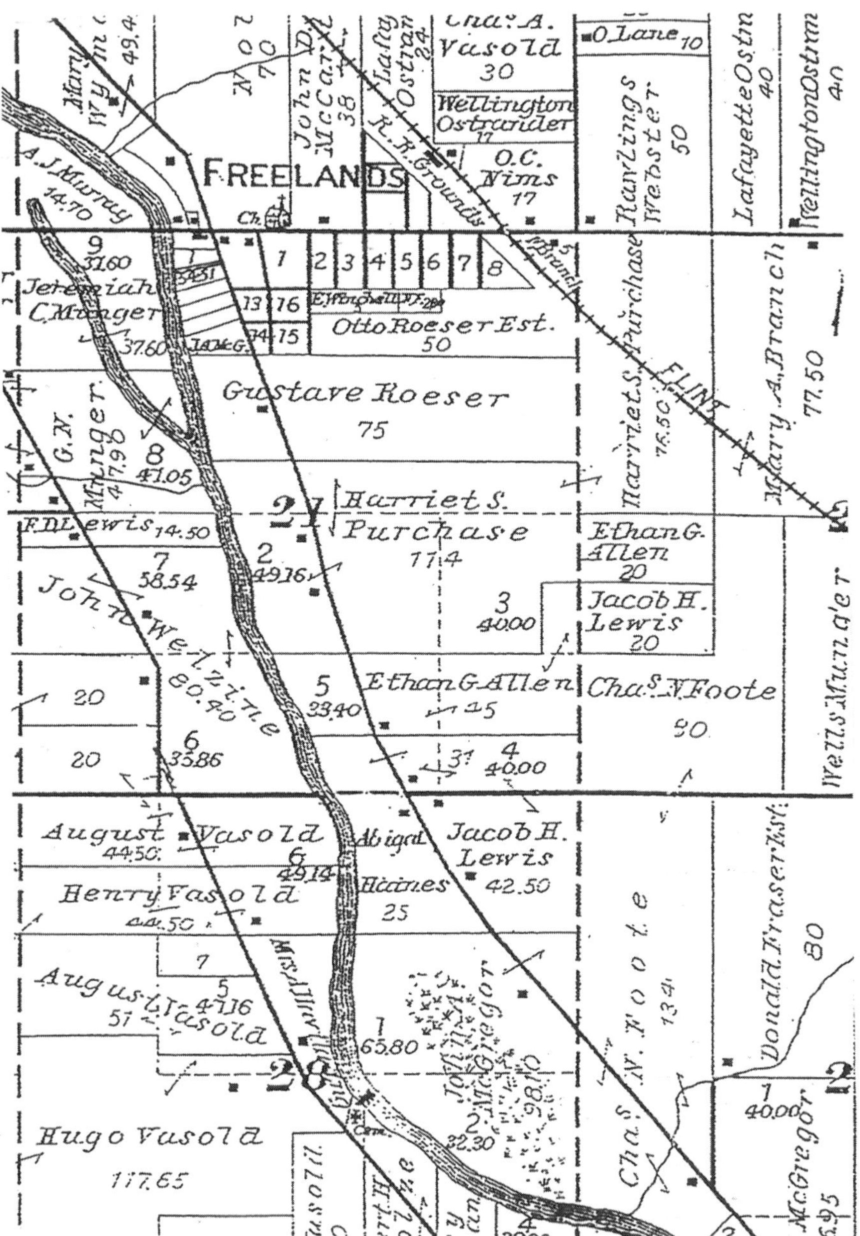

This section 21 is from the 1896 map of Tittabawassee Township. Jacob H. Lewis' farm is south of Pierce Road where Loretto developed. North of Pierce Road and east of Midland Road is the Lewis farm, Ethan Allen farm, and Purchase farm. Several other residents of Loretto lived along this stretch. Jefferson Jaquith had his house, store, and Post Office where E.G. Allen farm is shown. The small community was about one mile south of the village, which became Freeland. Vasold Collection

They could then sell their parcels for a profit.

Another group of buildings emerged just north of Loretto also east of the river. In 1867 it was platted as the Village of Tittabawassee. Mammy Freeland kept a hotel and tavern on the riverbank. The lumbermen, shanty boys, and river men frequented her hotel on their river journey between Midland and Saginaw. They referred to it as Freeland's. George Truesdale and his friends who lived in another cluster of backwoods houses worked a shady political maneuver to move the Jay Post Office to their Village of Tittabawassee in 1867. Jaquith then moved his Post Office to Roeser's Store. William Roeser served as postmaster from 1868 to 1885. The United States Government officially changed the name to the Freeland Post Office. The Pere Marquette Railroad also came closer to Tittabawassee than to Loretto, and it was called Freelands Station. The Village of Tittabawassee soon became known as Freeland, and Loretto eventually ceased to exist.

CHAPTER 4

FIRST SCHOOL DAYS

One night Gertie had great difficulty with her reading lesson for the next day. The troublemaker was the sentence: "I think I see the ship." (Not much sense to it anyway.) Over and over Mother worked and worked with her but each time with the same result: "I stink I see the shi." Gertie tried and tried with the same result. Kittie, not yet three years old, stood looking at her as over and over she said the same thing. When at last she thought Gertie had been saying naughty words long enough, she said "Well, now you'd better say a …hole!" Coming from a baby's innocent mouth, Mother had all she could do to keep from laughing and showing how shocked she was. When Floyd got mad, he used to use these pet words sometimes. So Kittie thought the time was ripe for their use now.

The next morning Gertie cried and didn't want to go to school. But she was persuaded to go and luck was in her favor that day. Someone else was called upon to read that pestiferous sentence. Gertie says to this day she can see how that sentence looked. Some impressions are lasting ones!

The two girls were almost inseparable and Kittie was so lonesome after Gertie started to school that the teacher, Mrs. Smith, said, "Let her go to school even though she is a little young." So the September before her fifth birthday pint-sized Kittie strutted off to school with Gertie and their double-cousin Louise who was one year three months older and just starting too. There didn't seem to be enough seats and desks that day so Louise and Kittie were given the seat fastened on the front of the front double desk with chairs for their desks. Here their supplies were kept: slate, slate pencil, slate rag, and *New Normal Primer.*

This is an early photograph of Louise Allen, born September 3, 1890. She and Kittie were double cousins and best friends. They lived in the same neighborhood, walked to school together, played together, and shared many childhood adventures.

How well Kittie remembered that first page in her reader. It seemed to be stamped indelibly upon her memory. While the reading matter was uninteresting to a five year old—she couldn't see why it mattered much whether the cup was in the box or on the box—nevertheless it was wonderful because it was her introduction to the printed page and became the symbol of knowledge gained from books, and made her feel very important.

How she liked the lilt of the song they learned: *Good Morning, Merry Sunshine.* Kittie wondered why they sang to Mary instead of to Kittie, but that didn't spoil the rhythm of the song. Then, too, they sang *Merrily the Cuckoo in the Glen.* She didn't know what a cuckoo was and anyway why should it be in glen? The only Glenn she knew was Glenn Branch and why should he have a cuckoo in him? It was sung in a nice fast tempo and she loved it.

Mrs. Smith's desk was upon a raised platform at the front of the room near which were two long recitation seats where children recited their lessons. And that is exactly what they did—recited or memorized their lessons and all the answers without ever asking why.

Kittie must have grown weary before the day was over as Mrs. Smith took her on her lap while hearing one class recite the lesson. Mrs. Smith was a pretty teacher, plump of figure, with dark hair, smiling gray eyes, full face with prominent front teeth. She was dressed in a black taffeta waist and black skirt. As the droning, monotonous sound of the recitation wore on, Kittie's head began to nod and soon became pillowed on her teacher's soft, plump bosom. She liked the feel of the pillow and the krinkly sound of the taffeta waist and

soon sailed off to slumber land.

At dismissal time to the commands—"Turn, Stand, Pass"—the children marched out of the room to the rhythmic clapping of Mrs. Smith's soft, rose-petaled hands as she stood clapping and smiling a goodnight to all.

Kittie went home with the determination she was going to be a teacher with puffy cheeks and large front teeth and was going to wear a black taffeta waist and skirt. She would smile and pat her hands together as her children filed past her at the end of the day. Kittie became a teacher all right, but the resemblance ended there!

Upon reaching home she arranged a row of chairs, got out her mother's old school bell and a book and pretended she was wearing a black taffeta waist and skirt. Her mother had been cutting corn off the cob for drying on an evaporator on top of the stove. Many of the kernels still held together—so slipping a row of them under her upper lip—presto! She looked just like her teacher with the pretty large teeth and the puffed-out cheeks. It was with a feeling of satisfaction that she stood smiling and clapping her hands together as her imaginary pupils filed past her and out the door. A Red Letter Day was closing in on a tired little girl—tired but happy! Kittie had had her first introduction to the halls of learning! Life would never be quite the same!

NOTES

Louise E. Allen was indeed a double cousin to Gertie and Kittie. Mary A. Lewis (Watson's sister) married Herbert L. Allen (Katie's brother). Louise's parents are the Aunt Mary and Uncle Herbert mentioned throughout the chapters. They lived in the same neighborhood. Louise was only a year older than Kittie. Kittie, Louise, and Gertie grew up together and engaged in the many childhood activities mentioned throughout this memoir.

CHAPTER 5

FIRST SCIENTIFIC EXPERIMENT

One very cold night on the way home from school Louise put the bail of her tin dinner pail in her mouth while fastening her mitten and the bail stuck to her tongue. Gertie said, "I'm going to see if my tongue sticks to this wire fence." It did! Why? They all wondered. Curiosity killed a cat but it only skinned a child's tongue! Not quite satisfied Gertie stuck her tongue on an iron bar on a big gate. It stuck all right. She spread her tongue as flat as she could and there on the iron bar she left the impress and a piece of her tongue.

Her tongue bled a little, and fearing she might bleed to death the three girls ran almost all the way home. Kittie still wasn't quite satisfied with the tests of their scientific experiment, so unknown to the family she went out the back door and stuck her tongue on the iron ring around the doorknob. Yes, the test proved that something wet would stick to a frosty metal surface! Both girls had to pass up the chilli sauce on their roast spareribs with dressing that night at supper. Thus ended the first experiment with tongue and steel!

Supper being finished out came Kittie's doll, which needed to have all its clothes changed. Mother had finished making a pretty white doll dress with ruffles and lace. And the doll must try on its dress. Kittie dearly loved a doll or a baby, and ever since her early days had said, "Well, I'm going to be a woman and have a baby." Gertie never cared very much for dolls but loved to dress the cat in doll clothes. She wanted something that could move around. And the Lewis home was never without cats and kittens. She was at her usual pastime—teaching school. From early childhood Gertie had declared: "I'm going to be a maid and teach school when I grow up."

In all her dreams of being a woman with a baby Kittie always imagined when she grew up and had a baby she would live in Grandpa's house across the road. And whenever she rocked her baby, she would sit in a rocker by the window where she could look over and see Mother. Mother was her idol and always figured in her plans. No doubt her many illnesses in babyhood and early childhood had formed an unusually strong bond between her and her mother—almost to the point of worship.

She always had a fear of getting lost from Mother. But Mother said, "I couldn't lose you because of your lock of white hair and that big mole on your back." That comforted her to a certain extent, but nevertheless, when out in a crowd she generally kept hold of her mother's skirt. For how were people going to see that mole under her dress? And usually the way her mother combed her hair that white lock didn't show. Better to be on the safe side—and hang on her mother's skirt!

Only once did she get lost—and that was at a picnic in Acker's Grove. For some unexplainable reason she walked some distance hanging on to the skirt only to discover when the skirt's owner looked around that she was hanging on to the wrong skirt. It was someone else's mother. But needless to say she found her mother without the two identification marks!

After an evening of teaching school, playing house and coloring a few black and white pictures in a storybook, bedtime came. All those clothes to take off and put on again in the morning. Clothes were laid over the backs of chairs and shoes near the heater so they wouldn't be so cold in the morning. Faces, necks, ears, arms, and hands to be scrubbed. How Kittie hated having her ears washed! It seemed as though Mother tried to put the whole washcloth in her ear. Then they slipped into their long outing flannel fleecy nightgowns. Then followed the little prayer:

Now I lay me down to sleep,
I pray Thee, Lord, my soul to keep;
If I should die before I wake,
I pray Thee, Lord, my soul to take. Amen

With a quick dash the girls hopped into bed where Mother had turned down the covers and placed hot flatirons wrapped in a towel to keep their feet warm. Gertie usually slept at the front. But if someone had died or something unusually scary had taken place, the first one to say, "Me to the back tonight!"

had that coveted place. For example: One night after Father had been to Freeland he came home and announced, "Well, John Brown, (a rural mail carrier) was found dead in his mail wagon today!" "Me to the back tonight!" came almost simultaneously from the lips of two frightened girls.

The girls seemed to think the one at the front might be taken but the one at the back left. In those days children had a terrible fear of dead people. They used to walk lightly when they had to pass the little undertaking building that stood right by the walk on Main Street. It was told that some boys had put one of the boys in a coffin in there and there was always that fear that one of them might have the same fate!

Another fear was when Mrs. Elsie Munger had diphtheria. She lived on Main Street where the girls had to pass her house to and from school. Before reaching her house they crossed the road, took a great deep breath and then held it and covered their mouths and noses until they got past the house. They must have thought those deadly germs had wings as well as feet. At any rate, the germs didn't catch up with them.

Next morning the same laborious process of dressing! Breakfast of slices of fried cornmeal mush fried on the pancake griddle in lots of butter and sugar to a crispy golden brown; sausages, sizzling hot from the heavy iron skillet; creamy oatmeal that had simmered all night on the back of the stove; homemade bread and butter, etc. No wonder everyone had to take their doses of sulphur and molasses in the spring to "thin their blood."

Then off to school for another adventure—but no more scientific experiments for the time being—at least until sore tongues had healed from the first one.

NOTES

The exact location of Acker's Grove is unknown. However, there may have been some kind of church or community picnic at Samuel P. Acker's 40-acre farm about two or three miles west of the Tittabawassee River near the Chapman Drain and the Indian Reserve Line. East side residents would need to cross the river on a raft and then travel by horse and wagon to the designated location. Chapter 25 gives another description and map of Acker's Pine Grove where the Freeland Fourth of July was celebrated. It was located on the west side of the river.

Although it is not shown on the map, there is another Acker house along the east side of the Tittabawassee River on the Midland Road. This is

This street scene of Midland or Main Street looking north was taken July 15, 1907. On the left side is a plank bridge over Roeser's Gully. Continuing on the left side would be Roeser's General Store with wood stacked on the side, Bishop's Hotel, which became Rodeitcher's, and then the Freeland Hotel, originally run by Mammy Freeland. On the right side from front to back would be Mrs. Gould's Hat Shop, Thurber's Restaurant, Barbarin Drug Store, Valley Telephone Office, and Dietiker's Store and Post Office. Kittie and Gertie walked this dirt road daily to and from school. Vasold Collection

mentioned in Chapter 14. The house would be in the Lewis' neighborhood, and there may have been a neighborhood or church gathering at this house.

During this time there were only three principal streets in Freeland—Main Street (M-47, Midland Road, or US-10), Washington Street (Freeland Road), and Church Street. The side streets south of Washington Street were only one block long. Depot Street was the only street north of Washington Street. All the roads and streets were unpaved dirt roadways and became muddy during wet weather.

The Munger Store was on Main Street, and Mrs. Elsie Munger ran this store. The two-story frame schoolhouse was located on the northeast corner of Church and Second Streets directly across from the Adventist Church. The Congregational Church was just behind the school on Third Street. The girls would have walked north up Main Street and passed by the Munger Store on their way to Church Street. Then they would continue east another two blocks until reaching their school on Second Street.

CHAPTER 6

WINTER CLOTHES OF THE '90's

Getting dressed for school in the winter was exasperating work. First came the long-legged, long-sleeved, fleece-lined underwear with the buttons up the entire front and its loose backdrop, which had to be hoisted up and buttoned on each side. Then, next came the underwaist to which the elastics were fastened, which buttoned in the back. Next, the long black cotton stockings had to be pulled up high after the long-legged underwear had been pulled tight around the ankles and wrapped around the legs—the difficult feat being to hold the wrapped underwear with one hand while pulling the stockings up with the other. If one were to let it slip, it was bound to roll up with the stocking making a second or third attempt necessary. Even at best the legs had a knobby, one-sided appearance. Then came those high leather shoes that had eyelets the first half way and little metal fasteners the last half into which and under the long shoelaces had to be laced and tied. Some shoes had buttons on one side, and these made little fingers sore when they couldn't find the buttonhook. Over the underwear went the pants that buttoned around the waist. Then there were at least two petticoats, which had to be buttoned. And then last was the wool dress buttoned down the back. Blessed the day of the zipper and the nylons! The Mother Hubbard or pinafore apron was worn to keep the dress clean. All this dressing took place out by the old Round Oak heater in the dining room.

Then for that breakfast that didn't stop to count its calories! Stacks of hot buckwheat cakes with maple or sometimes brown sugar syrup, sausages or fried ham, oatmeal with sugar and rich Jersey cream, and milk with a little hot tea or coffee to warm it after it had been nearly chilled to death standing in a milk crock on the shelf of that cold pantry.

Gertie and Kittie both wore their long hair in braids, so Mother had to comb and braid that each morning and tie on the big hair ribbons. Gertie wore her hair pulled back and puffed a little over her face and in one braid down her back. Because her face was so small, Kittie wore hers parted in the middle and in two braids down the back. Often these braids were crisscrossed and tied at the top with ribbons.

During a hurried trip to the little outhouse behind their house to see "Mrs. Jones" they didn't stop long enough to look at the magazines or newspapers that were piled in a box fastened on the wall in one corner. The seat which somewhat resembled (in appearance only) a narrow steam table with three holes had big, middle-sized, and small holes. It wasn't quite so bad if someone had been there first and warmed the seat a little. But if not, that first contact of warm flesh with ice-cold wood on a subzero morning was enough to spread goose pimples from head to foot.

Next came the wraps. First came a knitted or crocheted muffler which went around the neck and widened over the chest; then a heavy wool coat with several buttons; a warm bonnet, and if it were extra cold, a crocheted scarf or fascinator around the neck and up over the nose; leggings which buttoned up above the knees; and either rubbers or high galoshes with three or four buckles (hard for little fingers to manage over the knobby bungling underwear); and last of all, wristlets and mittens. The mothers' philosophy in those days was: "Keep bundled up."

The girls carried their lunch together so Gertie usually carried the dinner pail or lunch box. What good lunches emerged from that dinner pail! Sandwiches of ham, roast pork, fried or pressed chicken, headcheese, etc.; pickles; apples from the orchard; some kind of canned sauce—pears, plums, peaches; lemon tarts, cream cake, marble cake, pink and white cake (the envy of the other children); pumpkin, apple, lemon or mince pie; fried cakes or doughnuts; sugar cookies and molasses cookies—but not all on the same day. Oh, no! Mother varied her lunches every day and the children never knew what to expect from day to day.

Mother loved to cook and bake and had plenty of butter, buttermilk, milk, cream, eggs, lard, etc. to cook with besides all the vegetables, fruits, poultry, and pork. A flour barrel stood in the pantry, and there were always crocks of butter and lard. She always set a good table—her family was well fed—even if they maybe got more than their share of calories.

Chapter 7

Playing Hooky

Mrs. Campbell, a good friend of Mother's from Ingersol Township, had been at our house and left a treasure—a wallpaper sample book! She was a wallpaper sales lady and went about the country getting orders. Each year she discarded the old book for a new one. The book was about 18" x 24" and full of pretty designs on colored backgrounds. These made excellent decorations for picture books and valentines of the homespun variety. Best of all, it gave the girls the equivalent of two or more reams of drawing paper which wasn't available in the local stores.

And Father had just come from town with two boxes of wax crayons. What a perfect combination—drawing paper and colors for a child who loved to make pictures. A fisherman with a new rod and reel couldn't have been happier than the girls were.

It had snowed all day and had turned into one of those old-fashioned northeast blizzards during the night. Morning revealed great drifts everywhere. The fence posts were all wearing marshmallow caps. The snow had so covered up the old familiar sights that it looked like a strange world. Tracks in the road were completely obliterated. Schools weren't closed in the good old days when they didn't have to depend on buses. Mother thought it too bad a morning for the girls to start out. But Gertie was determined to go. As they started off, Mother said, "If you come to some bad drifts, you'd better come back home." Kittie mentally resolved it wouldn't have to be too big a drift.

Trudging along they had gone more than half way when Mr. Thomson said, "Well, girls, you'll never get through the drifts just the other side of my house. The drifts are up to your necks." All the way Kittie had been seeing

drifts with one eye and wallpaper and colors with the other.

Gertie said, "Well, I'm going to try to get through anyway." But Kittie said, "Well, I'm not because Ma said to come home if the snow is too deep. And Mr. Thomson ought to know." So they parted company. Kittie didn't want to see if Gertie got through so she didn't look back. Her two eyes now were fastened on home and wallpaper and colors! But when the wind blew across those gullies she half wished she'd stayed with Gertie for protection. She squatted on her heels and the wind blew her along on the slippery slope where it had blown much of the snow off, leaving a slippery, icy trail. She was afraid she'd be blown into the deep culverts. But she had no intention of being blown from those colors. When she reached home, Mother was frightened to think she had been out in that wind alone.

Practically all day long Kittie made pictures. Today her pictures would have been designated the creative type—expressing her own ideas and experiences. And though they were lacking in proportion and perspective, they made up for it in action and subject matter. Mother said she was the happiest child all day long—the only day she ever played hooky from school.

Gertie said she had found some of the drifts pretty deep but not quite up to her neck. And she was glad she hadn't missed school as so many other children had that day.

NOTES

There were several Thomsons in the surrounding neighborhood. This may have been David Thomson. He could have already been out on the roadway and met the girls as they trudged through the deep snow. The John Thomson family had been in Tittabawassee Township since 1834. David Thomson was John's son.

Chapter 8

Rain Barrels and Baths

Saturday night—bath night! With only outdoor plumbing preparations for bathing required considerable time and energy. In spring, summer, and fall a rain barrel stood under the eaves of the house, and a rain board slanting down into the barrel caught the rain running off the roof and sent it whooshing into the barrel.

Rainwater, like that from a cistern, was soft and capable of making good suds. So it was precious and used for washing and bathing. In the spring the water was alive with wrigglers—wrigglers the children called them—the larval stage of the mosquito, which lays eggs in stagnant water. Dozens of wrigglers came up in a pail dipped into the barrel, so this necessitated straining the water through a cloth—thus trapping all potential mosquitoes.

In summer droughts the barrel went dry and this made an ideal place for listening to one's echo. Putting the face down into the empty barrel and calling, the voice was greatly amplified as the airwaves vibrated and hit the sides and bottom and bounced back in the form of an echo.

There was a song that went something like this: "You can't holler down my rain barrel. You can't play on my cellar door." The cellar door referred to the outside doors that covered an outside stairway leading into the cellar. They were slanting doors that opened by folding back like the beds in the old camp trailer. The girls used to play on Uncle Guy and Grandpa's cellar doors.

But winter bathing really meant work. Big pans of snow, ice, and icicles were brought in and melted on the kitchen range. Some of this soft water was stored in the reservoir, which was a covered storage tank in the back of the stove. This kept quite hot if there was a fire in the stove.

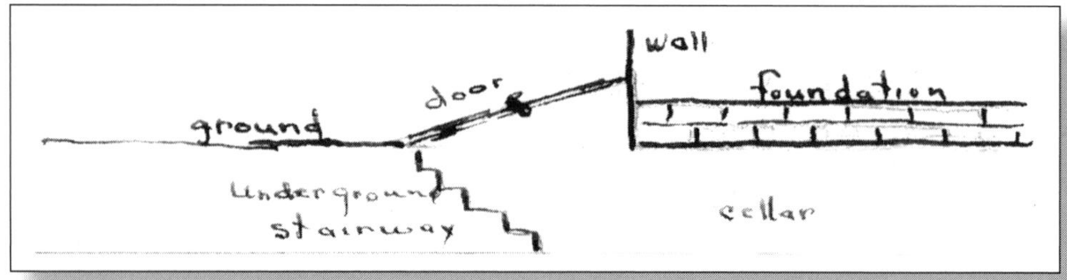

Saturday the big wash boiler was placed over the front burners and filled with water. The washtub was placed in the middle of the kitchen floor and served as the bathtub for the entire family.

Kittie and Gertie bathed first and got to bed—the family took turns according to age. Sometimes a large washbowl was used instead for sponge baths, which took more time but less water. At any rate they were as clean as whistles when these Saturday night ablutions were completed.

Clean clothes for Sunday were laid out for every member of the family. The girls went barefooted in summer so that meant washing their feet and legs every night. How they hated that—but that was a MUST—and there was no arguing about it.

Chapter 9

Sundays

Sunday morning, the year round, was a busy time. Chores to do—milk the cows by hand, feed and water them and the horses, pigs, and chickens. Milk had to be strained into earthen milk crocks and the milk pails and strainer washed. Father and Mother were kept busy. Sixty years later Gertie and Kittie could still remember vividly the disagreeable odor of warm milk and dishwater in those milky pails! Mother was the only one who liked warm milk fresh from the cow. The girls wouldn't drink it because it tasted "too cowy."

Then a hearty breakfast and getting ready for church and Sunday school, which began at 10:30 A.M. Old Nell, the old bay mare who was as gentle as a lamb, was hitched to the buggy and the family piled in. Nell had a peculiar gait—she traveled up and down as much as ahead so it took her quite awhile to get places but she was "slow but sure."

At church the family went inside and Father drove on to the church sheds where horses were tied in the different stalls.

Father was the best bell ringer the church ever had. He would pull the rope down on the Ding and sustain the Dong just long enough to make it interesting. Others seemed to ring it as though announcing a fire. One day little Kittie wanted to help ring the bell as she stood watching Father. He let her take hold of the rope while sustaining the Dong, and the next thing she knew she was way up near the ceiling and thought she was going right up into the steeple. Kittie was thrilled but not frightened because her father's hands were on the rope. The next instant her feet touched the floor. When Jesus said, "Except ye become as little children, etc.," He meant we should have faith in our Heavenly Father as a child has in its earthly father.

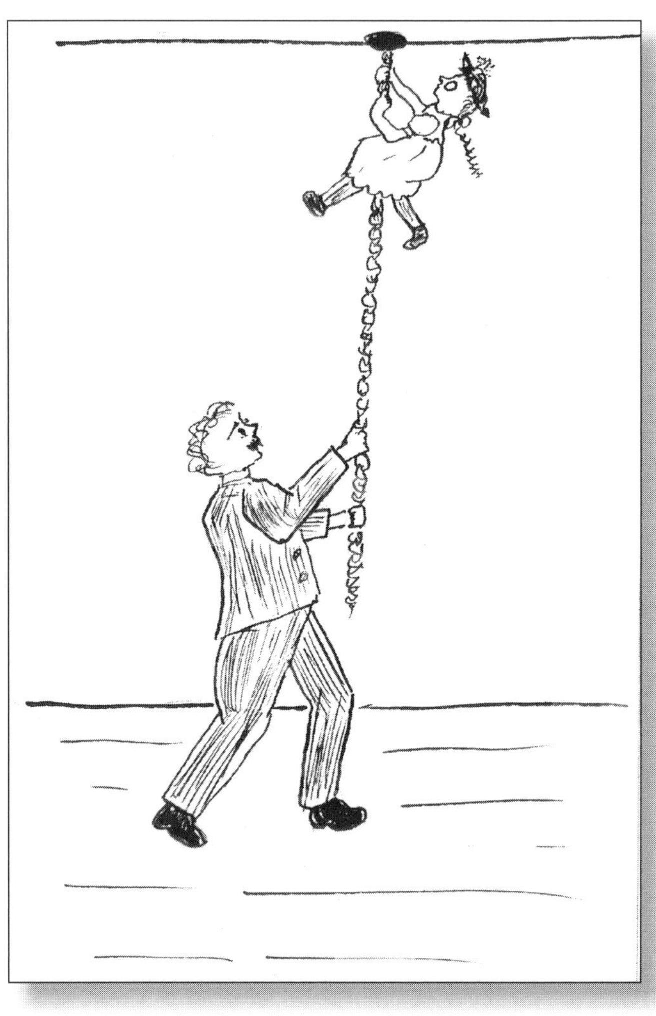

Soon the old standbys began arriving: Olmsteds, Steckerts, Mungers, Maidments, Stoddards, Thomsons, Prestons, Hawleys, Foxs, Arnolds, Bonstiels, Sarles, Wymans, Meekers, Nims, Turnbulls, Cubbages, Wilsons, Coles, Manwells, Bishops, Freelands, McPhersons, Loves, Adams, Mrs. C.A. Lewis, and others.

After an hour service and a short intermission for hand shaking and greeting one another, the Superintendent (Father) called the Sunday school to order by ringing the little call bell. (Kittie kept this same bell in her bell collection years later.) The chorister (Floyd when going with Ina) stood by the organ and led in singing those good old hymns: *Bringing in the Sheaves, When the Roll is Called up Yonder I'll be There, Anywhere with Jesus,* etc. Following the prayer the Sunday school lesson was read responsively, then the clanging of the call bell sent members off to their various classes.

Kittie and her classmates marched up on the rostrum where the primary class sat on adult chairs arranged in a circle. Their teacher, Miss Nancy Bonstiel, passed out little picture cards with the lesson story, questions, and

The Congregational Church was organized in 1891 and held services in the Adventist Church until this church was built in 1892 on Third Street behind the two-story frame schoolhouse. This view is the back of the church with horse sheds on the left side. An outhouse is right behind the church. Some members are playing croquet. Rev. Jacob Lewis is third from left side. The church site today is the Tittabawassee Township office's parking lot. Vasold Collection

golden text. As she told the story of "Nichodemus coming to Jesus by night," Kittie shivered a little to think of anyone being brave enough to go out alone at night. The picture showed Jesus and Nichodemus sitting on the parapet on top of a house with the night sky in the background. But somewhere during the story her attention became riveted on the black bangles dangling from the rim of Nancy's little black hat. As Nancy tried to take each child into her glances those black bangles bobbed incessantly and became a "study in black." Kittie decided then and there she would have black bangles on her hat some day.

She never saw Nancy except at church and Sunday school but Nancy wore the same hat Sunday after Sunday. Nancy was a dressmaker but not too prosperous. So as she sat watching the shiny bangles Kittie thought: "I wonder if that hat grew on her head. If it did, I wonder how she can sleep with all those things hanging from the brim." But her reverie was interrupted by the clanging of the call bell.

The secretary, prim Mrs. C.A. Lewis, stood up by her little table in front where she kept Sunday school supplies and took care of the records and read her report: the number present in each class; total present; amount collected in each class; and total amount. From the children it was usually a penny collection, so it perhaps amounted to the astronomical sum of $1.35 or thereabouts. As a matter-of-fact, Mrs. Lewis (no relation) always gave the impression that her job was the most important part of the Sunday school, and as she read her reports she looked the picture of importance. Kittie always sat admiring her two front teeth, which had wide gold bands across the bottom of each. Kittie decided that when she grew up, she was going to have long front teeth trimmed with gold! Years later when Kittie actually had some front ones with gold fillings, she wasn't so pleased about it.

The closing hymn—*Jewels, Tell Me the Story of Jesus, Take the Name of Jesus With You*—or some other favorite, a closing prayer, and then it was off for home and a big chicken dinner with mashed potatoes, biscuits and gravy and all the other fixing's topped off with lemon pie. Mother made the best lemon pie Kittie ever tasted. Maybe some popcorn or apples were eaten later in the evening.

Sunday being the Lord's Day, play activities took on a quieter more subdued color. The girls had a preacher grandfather to live up to, and their tomboy play was hardly in keeping with a preacher forebear. Father and Mother read and sometimes took a nap, and the girls looked at their Gospel Primer, read the parts they could, and talked about the pictures. This book was copyrighted in 1894 by Palmer and White and published by International Tract Society, Battle Creek, Michigan. This was the 11th edition—122nd thousand. Its purpose was "to present the truths of the Gospel in the form of simple stories, so that children and untrained minds can understand. While the stories are easy, so that children can read many of them they have been made so as to interest and instruct the older readers also."

The first few pages consisted of the A B C's and Word Method, Easy Lessons, and Lessons on Penmanship. Then beginning with the Creation and ending with the New Heaven and Earth were 120 pages of stories and illustrations from the Old and New Testaments.

Here is a reproduction of the first page:

A is for Adam who was the first man. (Slate Exercise)

The man for first Adam is

So God created man in His own image, in the image of God created

He him. Genesis 1:27

B is for Bethlehem, where Jesus was born. (Slate Exercise)

Was for is born where Jesus

Now when Jesus was born in Bethlehem of Judea, in the days of Herod the king, behold, there came wise men from the east to

Jerusalem.

Matthew 2:1

The last chapter is *"A Little Child Shall Lead Them*" taken from Isaiah 11:6 and the picture shows a very young child in tunic style dress leading a huge lion by the mane, surrounded by a tiger, wolf, sheep, lamb, cow, calf, bear, etc. all living together in peace. The illustrations were all in black and white, but with their imaginations the girls could see them in glowing colors: *Adam and Eve Leaving the Garden of Eden; The Israelites Gathering Manna; Moses Bringing Water From the Rock; Daniel in the Lions' Den; The Good Samaritan; Jesus Blessing the Little Children*—and all the others. These stories and illustrations were stamped indelibly upon their young minds. Kittie and Gertie have always been thankful they were raised in a Christian home.

Then Mother and Father had a big book, *The Pathway of Life,* by Reverend T. DeWitt Talmage, copyright vintage 1888, with 591 pages of religious and secular material. Kittie liked one picture in particular—*The Family Circle*—in which the father, mother, and four children are spending a pleasant evening together. The children are enthralled as the father is making a large shadow picture of a rabbit on the wall with his hands, and the baby is reaching out

This early 1900s photo of the east side of Main Street shows the Bank in the distant corner, Dietiker's Store and Post Office, Valley Telephone Office, Barbarin Drug Store, Thurber's Restaurant, and Mrs. Gould's Hat Shop. Shown in front of the Drug Store are Mr. Barbarin, Rhea, Mr. Winslow, and Ottelia Vasold. Vasold Collection

gleefully to get the large rabbit on the wall. (Father and Mother used to entertain their own family the same way by making rabbits, horses, etc.)

Then there was Joan of Arc at the Stake and other martyr pictures. One that made a great impression was a beautiful chubby baby and its black cat floating along on the floodwater in a sturdy cradle—entitled *The Flood—Safe While Jesus Watches.* Playing with its hands, its eyes on the cat, the baby is unaware of any danger. Another illustration in bright COLORS was: *Persecution of The Christians at Rome by Nero* showing the arena with its many galleries filled to overflowing with spectators. At the right foreground a group of about thirty martyrs are on their knees and an old white-bearded, white-haired saint stands in their midst with his eyes lifted to heaven in prayer. In the center a large, sleek lion is hungrily moving toward the martyrs, and at the left three more lions are looking from the pit where a trapdoor has been raised. There were many good Bible illustrations.

Some very touching secular pictures were: *The Little Orphan's Dream, Watching for the Father and Husband That Will Come No More, The Empty Place, The Parting, The Widower and His Children, Motherless,* and many others equally touching! Morbidness seemed to characterize the literature and

illustrations of the times.

Since the youngsters of sixty years ago survived these harrowing pictures, certainly *Have Gun, Will Travel, Shotgun Slade, Coronao 9, Wagon Train, The Cisco Kid,* etc. won't damage the minds of today's children and youth too extensively if they have a Christian home and receive love and nurture of the right kind. The sad part is that so many homes today are lacking in this, stressing too much the material things of life, which, after all, are so very transient. In a happy Christian home these morbid impressions seemed to roll off like water from a duck's back.

Chores again, then back to church for the 7:30 P.M. service, which was evangelistic in its message. Then home again and a lunch of bread and milk or hot mush and milk which was a great favorite. The leftovers could be fried in hot butter and sugar the next day. Sunday had been a full day and a happy one.

Time for the new spring hats. So up to Mrs. Gould's shop one Saturday evening to make the all-important decisions. Gertie said, "I want a hat with something on it that will stand up and wiggle." Mrs. Gould's sister, Mrs. Em Mills, said, "Well, we'll see that you have something that stands up and wiggles!" The next day in church Gertie saw to it that it wiggled. Mother was so annoyed she felt like shaking her. She said Gertie didn't sit still one minute but bobbed her head first this way and then that way. Everyone could see that she had something that wiggled! And Gertie was fully satisfied with her new hat.

Kittie and Gertie were always fascinated with large hats, even those that did not wiggle! Their large hats are lavishly decorated with flowers, the style of the day. The three young ladies from left to right—Kittie, Louise, and Gertie—are standing on the steps of the Congregational Church along with the minister. Photo taken before 1913.

NOTES

The Congregational Church was organized during the winter of 1890-1891 and then held its first public services on February 23, 1891 in the Adventist Church. There were 21 members. The church was built in 1892 on Third Street behind the two-story frame schoolhouse. The Adventist Church was across the street from the school on Second Street. Membership had increased to 135 members by 1893. The Congregational Church was a community church since many of the long-time residents attended this church. Kittie's grandfather, Jacob H. Lewis, had been a Methodist circuit rider before becoming pastor of this church from 1892 to 1897. The Lewis Family remained faithful members of the Congregational Church for years.

Kittie taught Sunday school, served as clerk and treasurer, and was the pianist and organist for 50 years in this Church. The Church still existed in 1950. The exact date when it disbanded is unknown. Then, Kittie joined the Freeland Baptist Church. The Congregational Church site today is the Tittabawassee Township office's parking lot. Mrs. Gould's milliner shop would have been on Main Street in Freeland.

A photo of the handsome teenage Floyd Lewis during the 1890s shows his naturally wavy hair.

Chapter 10

A Visit from the Lewis Clan

A letter from Unionville brought the good news that Uncle Will, Aunt Cora, Winnie, Leon, Arthur, and Willie Lewis were coming to spend a two-week Christmas vacation with the family. That was before any additions had been added to the house. How could three small bedrooms sleep four adults and seven children?

Mother always was a good manager and had a reserve fund of ambition. Upon arrival Uncle Will always demanded, "Bring on the chicken and cream cake!" Father met them at the depot with the sleigh, and a bountiful supper was in readiness when they arrived. Coats, leggings, mittens, and galoshes were strewn here and there—over chair backs, on the beds, on the floor! The house boasted no closets, but an entry or little hall at the foot of the stairway had several hooks for wraps. The house was fairly bulging at the seams.

Willie was a dainty, pretty baby in a pink outing flannel dress. Gertie fell in love with him and became his second mother. Father's younger sister, Aunt Stell, had died leaving a little boy, Earl. For awhile he stayed at Grandpa's but spent most of his days with Floyd, whom he worshiped. Floyd went over to Grandpa's to sleep with Earl. The three girls slept in the back bedroom. Uncle Will and Aunt Cora were in the front bedroom, and the two boys slept on the floor and Willie in the cradle.

Aunt Cora was one who never let housekeeping worry her, and wet diapers were apt to be thrown almost anywhere. This bothered Mother more than feeding the entire crowd. Morning brought eleven hungry mouths to the breakfast table where buckwheat pancakes and homemade sausage disappeared like the proverbial rabbit in the magician's hat.

A coasting party on the Haines hill across the road was the order of the day for the young fry of all ages. Cousins Earl and Louise came to join the fun. Being short of sleds the boys made some from barrel staves. Sometimes when the sleds were given enough momentum they spun down the slippery hill, on down the river bank and whooshed out on the Tittabawassee River, which was frozen to a depth of several inches.

A few hours later weary muscles and sharpened appetites sent the gang trooping back to headquarters where a steaming hot dinner of roast pork, stuffing (dressing), mashed potatoes, squash, pickles, homemade bread and butter, jelly, pumpkin pie, and milk filled the aching voids and furnished enough energy to carry them through until supper time.

Soon Floyd was at his favorite pastime—dancing a jig beside the stove in the dining room. He was hoeing it down with all the vim and vigor characteristic of a boy his age. Sometime later he actually jigged a hole through the carpet.

Earl had dashed up the stairs two steps at a time to the attic where he wholeheartedly was treading Father's jigsaw making it sound like a threshing machine. Leon and Arthur were wrestling over by the stair door, but Leon downed Arthur—bumping his head on the doorknob, which made Arthur, send up a lusty yell and broke up the wrestling match. Gertie was walking around carrying her beloved Willie darling. Earl was teasing Winnie in the front room. And Kittie was playing with her doll and dishes in the bedroom.

The boys declared the hill wasn't slippery enough so they carried water over there, pouring it on the packed snow. Next morning the sight of that slippery hill was rich reward for all their efforts. The hill wore an icy crown! The barrel stave sleds could speed down the hill—down that icy incline as well as the ones with steel runners. The boys conceived the idea of rolling a barrel of old broken crockery and bottles, etc. down the hill. All went as scheduled until Leon slipped, falling under the heavy barrel. He came up with a broken nose, which put a crimp in the fun the rest of the day. After that his nose was always a little bit crooked.

Mother was kept busy replenishing the larder. Once in a while Grandma came over with a plate of cookies, but she said she couldn't have them at her house. Aunt Mary said she wouldn't have them either so it was up to Aunt Katie to see the venture through.

After two weeks of hectic days and wakeful nights all but Mother piled into the sleigh to take them to the depot. The train was late and it was dark when the clanging bell of the locomotive signaled that the Will Lewis clan was on its way home.

Arriving home, the symbol of peace after the storm, Gertie broke into tears crying, "I won't see Willie any more." Mother remarked rather dryly, "Well, I won't mourn if I don't see Willie or the rest of them for a while!" Life had been filled with excitement and fun, but it was good to get back to normal again.

That last morning has always been remembered by the girls. Winnie was having a hard time finding her own stockings in the array of many pairs around the stove. She picked up first one and then another, smelling of each one until she identified her own by smell. Then she hastened to put them on—a look of happy satisfaction settling upon her hitherto worried face.

CHAPTER 11

THE EBONY QUARTET

One winter a group of black men and women came to the Congregational Church to furnish music at some special evening meeting. This was the first time all the children had ever seen dark-skinned people—their smooth ebony skin, larger lips and snowy-white teeth made a big impression upon all the young children. Kittie was fascinated with the large man who sang bass. Rolling his eyes, his big bass voice went down, down until it matched the lowest note or key on the organ as the group sang, *No moah peck o' salt foah me, No moah, no moah!* And how they did let out on *Jordan River and you must go across.* These are the only songs Kittie could remember for years afterwards. But this new kind of entertainment gave birth to a new kind of recreation for Gertie, Kittie, and Louise.

Gertie's chum, Murl Freeland, practically lived at the Lewis house and Louise was there most of the time too. Lampblack was available and cheap. Just light a kerosene lamp; turn the wick up high and the result was a blackened lamp chimney. Holding a plate over lighted matches gave good results also. But if more black was needed the bottom of the old three-legged iron kettle supplied it. Transferring this black to four eager faces, it was a matter of only a few minutes before four full-fledged black little girls emerged. Murl was large anyway and dressed in Father's old clothes padded in the right places. She became the father of the ebony quartet. Gertie, in Mother's old calico wrapper, claimed motherhood, while Louise and Kittie of smaller stature had to be content to be their offspring.

Many evenings were spent at Uncle Guy's—entertaining him, Aunt Josie and the hired girl, Jennie Emery. Uncle Guy's avoirdupois measured over 200 pounds, and his hearty, booming laugh matched his weight. Having no children of his own his nephew and nieces rated high in his esteem. They'd sing so loudly it was a miracle their lungs remained intact without bursting. Perspiration mingled with lampblack and the louder Uncle Guy laughed the more fortissimo the singing became. Then the four pooped-out girls would rub their padded stomachs, roll their eyes upward and beg for cookies. Their begging always brought a plate of caraway cookies from the well-stocked pantry, which was a step higher than the dining room.

Uncle Herbert, Aunt Mary, Father, and Mother enjoyed the singing quartet as much as the other spectators did.

There being no cleansing creams in those days, that lampblack stuck to faces as bark to a tree. It took a lot of washing with soap and water to remove all traces. Quite often the quartet would leave some black under the eyes and above the upper lip—so it was a cadaverous looking quartet that the rays of the morning sun shone upon.

Another frequent pastime was playing tramp. It was quite common in those days to have a tramp in ragged clothes stop at the door and beg for food. Mother would always hand out some food. She always thought she might be entertaining some angels unawares. It has been said that tramps had some way of letting other tramps know which houses would show hospitality. At any rate they all found their way to the Lewis door where they had a welcome hand out.

One day in the middle of the forenoon a dirty old tramp came along. Mother had emptied the coffeepot but she made a big generous sandwich or two and took them on a plate to the front porch where he was waiting. Then he asked for coffee. Mother said she didn't have any coffee made. "Well," he said, throwing down the sandwiches, "If I can't have coffee, I won't eat!" and he went off muttering to himself. Mother thought he was rather particular for a beggar. Making coffee at that time of day in summer would have meant starting up a fire in the wood range.

One day Kittie dressed up in some of Floyd's old clothes, put a mask over her face and a cap on her head and knocked at Grandma's door. She had the impression that with her face disguised Grandma would think she was a big man. As Grandma opened the door, Kittie asked, "Would you have anything

for a hungry tramp to eat?" "Hoo, hoo, hoo!" laughed Grandma almost convulsed at the pathetic sight of the hungry beggar. Some sugar cookies were forthcoming and the half-filled tramp was on his way again. Seeing Louise a little way ahead he stalked her for a short distance. Then fearing she wasn't going to look around, he cleared his throat in a gruff fashion. Looking around Louise gave a shrill shriek and yelled, "Oh, Aunt Katie! Aunt Katie!" and tore through a gap in the fence losing her shoes as she ran—one in the ditch and the other in the tansy bed. Kittie had been pursuing her in hot haste, and Louise was so frightened that she didn't recognize her until Kittie laughed and lifted her mask—the one Jack Doran gave her. That homely dark mask was enough to scare even Superman.

NOTES

Murl Freeland was obviously a relative of Mammy Freeland, who ran the Hotel by the riverbank on the southwest corner of Main and Washington Streets. She may have been Mammy's granddaughter. Murl may have lived on the corner of Washington and Fourth Streets as shown on the village map. Jack Doran was a neighbor and probably a descendant of William Doran who had purchased property in 1881 in the former little community of Loretto. The map shows a Peter Doran farm on Pierce Road, only a short distance from the Lewis farm. The circumstances under which Jack Doran gave her the homely mask are explained in Chapter 15.

A tansy bed was actually an herb garden. The tansy was a common weedy herb looking like a daisy having an aromatic odor with bitter tasting leaves. The 1800s people raised their own herbs and used them for cooking and medicinal purposes.

Ethan G. Allen III with his first wife, Catherine Mary Hubbard, taken during pre-Civil War era. She was born 12/24/1819 and died 2/6/1865. Nine children were born during this marriage. The family came to Freeland in 1857. Katie Allen was the only child born in Tittabawassee Township in 1860. All others were born in the East.

Chapter 12

Grandpa Allen, Cart and Coffin

When Kittie was about seven (1898) her Grandpa Allen, Mother's father, came from Friendship, Wisconsin with bag and baggage to live with the family. When Mother (Katie) was about seven (1867) he had remarried 46-year-old Olive Tarbox, a typical old maid. The next year they had a baby, Uncle Jesse. Olive was mean and hateful, making life miserable for Grandpa's children. After about three years she induced him to sell his good farm in Tittabawassee Township where land was rich and to buy a farm in Wisconsin where the soil was poor (near her folks). They took Uncle Herbert and Katie, the two youngest, with them where they lived for seven years.

Olive was very suspicious, quarrelsome, and garrulous. She shamed Katie for sitting on her father's lap. "A big girl seven years old sitting on her father's lap!" she would say in disgust. She caused Katie many humiliating experiences.

Katie's mother had died of pneumonia when she was four (1865), the youngest of nine children. Her name was Catherine Hubbard. So while our Grandma wasn't Old Mother Hubbard, she was Grandma Hubbard.

Aunt Nettie, 18 years older, was teaching school at Munger School across the Tittabawassee River. Aunt Ellen also was a teacher. Uncle Guy was an enlisted soldier in the Civil War. And Aunt Pollie and Uncles Josiah, John, Herbert, and Katie (Mother) were at home. Uncle Ephraim had stayed with relatives in Jamestown, New York when the family moved here.

After her mother's death, Katie was bossed first by one and then the other. Her father humored her but while the older sisters loved her they often grew impatient with her. She was an extremely imaginative child and could entertain herself by the hour. (Kittie inherited that tendency from her.) One day when

Aunt Ellen was stirring up a cake, Katie kept teasing. In desperation Aunt Ellen plopped a whole teaspoonful of ginger in her mouth. Fate was on her side or she would have choked to death. She turned red, then cerise and finally purple as she coughed and gasped for breath. Aunt Ellen was frightened out of a year's growth by her thoughtless act. For some time remorse made her extra nice to little Katie. She even bought her a new dress.

The family wanted to send a picture of Katie to Uncle Guy. So they began to talk to her about taking a trip to the city. She had little idea of a city but imagined it was something nice. It was a cold day, and she had to wear a veil over her face—a blue veil at that!

By the time her tintype was taken, Katie was tired and cross. She said, "You said I was going to see the city, and all I've seen is buildings and houses—and they were all blue!" Uncle Guy must have treasured the picture as he carried it with him all through the War. (It is in Kittie's possession now.) Katie is snuggled up close to Aunt Nettie and has a very cross expression on her face as she leans her head against her big sister. The family laughed when they saw the picture and Katie tried to scratch it out. These marks show on the tintype but they didn't happen to touch the faces. (Let's digress a little here to give you some of Mother's early background.)

Olive made Katie do a certain amount of knitting every day before she could play. She must have had a very unhappy life herself as she had a grudge against the whole world. Jesse's wife, Agnes, told Kittie and Gertie the summer they visited in 1925 that the last thing Olive did before she died was to make a face at her. She had the type of face that would sour a pan of milk or stop a clock at one glance.

Now to continue with Grandpa—he was given the front bedroom where his trunk and belongings were stored. He divided his time between Mother and Uncle Guy, making our house his headquarters, but often eating dinner or supper at Uncle Guy's. This plan gave spice to his life. Aunt Mary was such a person to storm and scold that he didn't spend as much time with good Uncle Herbert.

One day Grandpa gave Gertie and Kittie each a dime to buy something they wanted. Characteristic of all children that money had to be spent at once before it burned a hole in their pockets. On Saturday they walked to Freeland

This was a photo taken of Ethan G. Allen III during his later years.

where they divided their time between Dietiker's and Elsie Munger's Stores. It was around Christmas time so the stores were stocked with various trinkets.

Indecision—"Which shall I buy?" First to one store—"I think I'll buy this"—then back to the other—"I think I'd rather have this one." After an afternoon of wavering and indecision Gertie's dime finally left her hand and she became the proud owner of a little raffia sled with hand painted celluloid cover and underneath the cover—a bottle of perfume—all for a dime! Not "My Sin" exactly—but a perfume with a far-reaching, overpowering, exotic fragrance??

Kittie at last decided upon the covered frosted glass dish with a painted water scene of a sailboat and two gulls flying over the water. It was 3" x 3" x 3" with four legs and four little nubs on the corners of the cover. It became her keepsake box in which she kept her special treasures—a bent hairpin the train had spread out flat when she had put it on the railroad track; a tiny turtle whose head and legs wiggled whenever it was picked up; and a square piece of thick glass with a bubble in the center. Floyd had given her the last two objects. Then later she added a picture she made after playing at Louise's one summer night. Uncle Herbert had mowed the yard and stacked the hay in little haycocks to dry. It was now nice and dry, and Louise and Kittie were having as much fun as a bushel of monkeys when Aunt Mary discovered them. She stood there, hands on her hips, yelling, "That's right! Scatter it all over the yard!" They had been running and diving into it pretending they were at the beach.

Another time Grandpa gave the girls another dime each and this time Gertie bought a little square dish with pansies painted on the cover. Kittie bought a small hand painted cup and saucer, probably Bavarian, but there was no name on the bottom to designate where made. This wasn't required of countries until the time of McKinley's administration about 1900.

Pack peddlers used to go through the country, opening their mysterious bags to exhibit shoelaces, pins, needles, combs, suspenders, necklaces, and what have you. Mother never could turn anyone away, so at least one of his treasures found sweet haven in her house. One such peddler had some very alluring necklaces, and seeing the girls' eyes grow big with wonder Grandpa bought three of them—blue and gold beads for Gertie, and black and gold for both Louise and Kittie as there were no more blue ones.

Clay roads being what they were in the '90's almost every farmer had a two-wheeled cart for use in the spring when roads were almost impassable. Playing with this cart became a favorite pastime in the summer. Gertie, Louise, Kittie and often Murl Freeland took turns being the horse. Grandpa was 80 years older than Kittie and the girls conceived the idea of taking him over to Uncle Guy's in the morning and bringing him home at night. Grandpa sat in that cart as proud and straight as a king on his throne. The seat of the cart was hinged in front but loose at the back like a box cover. When the shafts or "fills" were dropped suddenly, that seat would flop up from the back, but Grandpa seemed oblivious of his precarious position. The little female horses always took extra precaution whenever he was in the cart, so he was always delivered and returned intact. He really looked forward to his daily ride. Mother must have had more confidence in her harum-scarum daughters than Kittie had had after she had grown up.

One dry dusty summer day Murl was the horse taking Gertie and Kittie for a ride. Everything went well until Murl was trotting ankle deep in the dust in the gully between Uncle Guy and Grandpa's houses. The stifling dust came up in her face almost suffocating her. She dropped the fills. The seat flew up. Gertie was thrown out over a wheel and Kittie over the dashboard—both landing in the dust, angry but unhurt. They told Murl what they thought of her but she said, "I couldn't help it—I thought that dust would choke me." Fortunately it was the girls instead of Grandpa. They wouldn't have trusted him in Murl's care.

Grandpa was very fond of his grandchildren and they of him, but he thought Mother was too easy with them. Their only household duties—washing dishes and drying them and making their bed—being done, they were free for a day of play. "I should think you'd make those long-legged girls do some work," he would say. But Mother wasn't going to have their childhood days spoiled as hers were. Her philosophy was "Let them have a good time while they're young. They'll grow up soon enough and have plenty of time for work then."

The girls heartily agreed with her philosophy. Grandpa had learned quite a few Indian words and expressions and some of their rhythmic songs and dances, so he used to entertain the children with some of them. Mother said as a young man he was a very good dancer. His favorite hymn seemed to be *From Greenland's Icy Mountains.* He wanted Kittie to name her doll "Sibyl"—a name that she didn't like at all. She named it "Kathleen" but always called it "Sybil" whenever he was around. Just a matter of diplomacy! He named Louise's "Imogene."

Just before going to bed Grandpa and Kittie often played Tag. He had said, "All right, Kittie, you got my Tag last tonight, but I'll get yours in the morning." His trunk was packed; his clean clothes were laid out; he had taken his bath. Tomorrow Mother was going to take him to Aunt Ellen's in Saginaw for a few weeks. Since Uncle John's death Aunt Ellen had been very lonesome and she wanted Grandpa for a while. Grandpa was excited about it but at the same time rather depressed. He felt close to Mother and was happy where he was.

About 5 o'clock in the morning he called, "Katie! Katie!" Hurrying to his bedroom, Mother found him in great pain—a heart attack. "Katie, I'm a gonner this time," he said. Awakened by the commotion other members of the family crept stealthily into the front room. "My God, he's dying!" the girls heard their mother say. And soon the solemn words, "He's gone."

"Me to the back tonight," said both girls in the same breath—meaning that the one who said it first could sleep at the back of the bed.

As was the custom long ago a napkin or cloth was brought from under the chin and tied over the head of a dead person to keep the mouth closed. Eyelids were pressed down—sometimes weighted with pennies—the origin of the expression "so greedy he'd steal the pennies from a dead man's eyes." Then a sheet was drawn up covering the body and face. Father went to Freeland to get Mr. Johnson, the undertaker, and Floyd was dispatched to Saginaw to take the sad news to Aunts Ellen and Pollie.

In due time Mr. Johnson arrived and did all the embalming right there at the house. He kept making trips through the house to dispose of the bloody-looking substance he had drawn from Grandpa's veins. And oh, that unforgettable smell of formaldehyde! To this day that odor is always associated with his death. After this lengthy process he lay peaceful and still shrouded under a winding sheet. The undertaker hung a black, gloomy-looking crepe on the door.

Aunts Ellen and Pollie arrived in a few hours swathed in mourning garments and veils in memory of Uncle John's death. The girls were chilled to the bone with all this black mystery of death.

Before the funeral Grandpa lying in a black cloth-covered coffin was placed in the front room, with only a commercial sheaf of wheat on the coffin. Flowers for funerals were almost unknown then. (Kittie thought she wanted a lot of them at hers.)

After a prayer and short service at the house, the funeral procession proceeded to the church for the lengthy funeral service. The hearse was enough to make a dead man shudder. Glass was on all sides with black draperies all drawn on the inside. At each corner of the top were fancy knobs or very ornate posts with a high one in the center. This was drawn by a team of beautiful black horses.

As the organist played a dirge all the mourners (relatives) walked slowly up the center aisle. Then a mixed quartet sang *Sometime We'll Understand.* A prayer followed by another song—usually *Nearer My God To Thee*; then a long sermon and remarks about the deceased followed by a third song—often *Abide With Me*—another prayer and then the tramp, tramp, tramp of feet as all in the congregation, one row at a time, marched around to doleful organ music

The Freeland Band leads this grand Decoration Day parade down Main Street (Midland Road, M-47 today) to the Pine Grove Cemetery in the 1890s. It was preceded by a patriotic ceremony with music, speeches, and prayers to honor those local Civil War heroes who gave their lives during the War. A large procession similar to this one, with a team of beautiful black horses pulling the hearse, paraded from the Congregational Church down Midland Road to the cemetery to lay Grandpa Allen to rest in June 1902. Vasold Collection

to "review the remains" as the undertaker called it. Finally the long, slow ride in horse-drawn carriages to Pine Grove Cemetery where Grandpa was finally laid to rest.

Having a dead person in the house for three days, even though it was dear Grandpa, was a strain on everybody, especially on Gertie and Kittie. They were afraid to go to sleep at night—even at the back of the bed. They had heard at school about ghosts and expected maybe Grandpa's ghost would be wandering about. Then, too, when a dead body was lying in a house neighbors and friends always came and sat up all night, having a lunch about midnight to relieve their weariness. They visited in low tones, but with the shock and excitement sleep was almost impossible. Mother was somewhat of a sleepwalker, so she was afraid to go to sleep for fear she'd get out of bed and walk out into the room where neighbors were sitting. She started one night but Father grabbed her just in time. At that time there were no doors on the bedrooms—just drapes.

Everybody breathed a sign of relief when the last rites were over and they could settle down to normal family living again. For a while the girls were afraid to sleep in the front bedroom. A ghost might be lingering there still.

Murl's little cousin, Fern Brown who lived next-door to her, died and her funeral was in the Adventist Church. Several of her little friends sat up in the balcony, and little Fern in a small white coffin was carried in by six girls of Murl's age, all dressed in white. This, too, made a profound impression and for some time set the stage for a large part of the children's play. "Let's play funeral" became the theme song of not only the girls but also the entire school group.

One summer day Inez Hoyt gave a party at her house. By unanimous consent the group decided to play funeral with Inez' little doll as the corpse. Mrs. Hoyt had some beautiful yellow roses and, unknown to her, practically every rose was picked and sacrificed to Death. Gertie played the funeral march on Inez' little toy piano. The mourners marched in in tears. A few did the singing. Someone preached the sermon. Then all marched solemnly around for a last look at "the remains." The pallbearers carried her out in the backyard. And while one of the girls was digging a grave she brought the hoe down on Flora King's hand, which had gotten in the way as she was pulling the loosened dirt to one side—and a cut finger diverted the attention from the remains for a few minutes. But finally the body was buried and her grave smothered with yellow roses. Everyone must have relished the cake and ice cream after all those harrowing ceremonies. Everyone left, telling Inez what a good time they had had!

And still the girls hadn't quite gotten funerals out of their systems. Because she was the smallest Kittie was always the corpse, lying very still in the wash boiler—doubled up like a jack knife, her hands folded across her breast, as was the custom then. The other girls "mourned" as they stood looking at her. Then she was carried out and let down into a ditch with such a jolt that she suddenly came to life, letting out a lusty yell. But happy, healthy children can't stay morbid very long and soon they were back at their tomboyish play. But not before a careful search of the attic failed to bring to light any mourners' veils or even a remnant of black cheesecloth. But with Kittie's imagination

a piece of white cheesecloth or an old lace curtain could be transformed into a mourning veil as readily as the fairy godmother could change Cinderella's pumpkin into a golden coach. On the edge of the heavy mourning veil was a deep band of heavier black material to designate it from other veils. And the veil dropped low over the face to partially hide the sorrowful faces from the gaze of onlookers who liked to see "how they took it."

NOTES

Ethan G. Allen III was born in New York State on May 30, 1813 and was a direct descendant of Ethan Allen (1738-1789) who was the leader of the Green Mountain Boys during the American Revolutionary War. The Green Mountain Boys took their name from the Green Mountains in Vermont. In 1775 Ethan Allen and Seth Warner led these soldiers when they seized Fort Ticonderoga and Fort Crown Point on Lake Champlain from the British. In 1777 they won the Battle of Bennington in Vermont. Before and after the War they fought for Vermont's opposition to territorial governance by New York. Vermont became the 14th State of the Union in 1791.

Ethan G. Allen came to Tittabawassee Township after 1857. He had nine

This is the Allen Family plot at Pine Grove Cemetery where Grandpa Allen was laid to rest. The graves from left to right are: Mother—Catherine, died 1865; Father—Ethan, died 1902; Son—Ethan G., died 1919; Wife—Josephine, died 1907; Son of J.H. & B. Allen, died 1/04/1881, 9 months, 2 days old. Ederer Collection

children by his first wife, Catherine Mary Hubbard, who died on February 6, 1865. Katie (Kittie's Mother) was the youngest child born on June 11, 1860 in Tittabawassee Township. Ethan died on June 2, 1902 and was laid to rest next to his wife Catherine. Next to him are his son, Ethan G. (Uncle Guy) who died in March 1919 and his wife, Josephine Jaquith Allen, who died in 1907. The grave of a nine-month-old baby of J.H. and B. Allen who died in 1881 is next to Josephine.

Charles Dietiker's store, grocery, and post office was on the southeast corner of Main and Washington Streets in the Freeland Village. His store would have been very near Mrs. Elsie Munger's store. The girls went back and forth between the two stores to decide what to buy with their dimes.

Charles Dietiker's Grocery and Crockery Store was on the southeast corner of Main & Washington Streets. He also served as Postmaster from 1897 to 1908. This was the store where Kittie and Gertie spent their dimes from Grandpa Allen. They also shopped at Elsie Munger's Store nearby. Vasold Collection

Chapter 13

Kittie Becomes a Wage Earner

Grandma Lewis was allergic to dust and had bad attacks of asthma at times. Housework didn't seem to be her forte anyway. Eight-year-old Kittie (1899) was engaged to do the sweeping and dusting once a week on Saturday.

She swept the carpets in the big front room, bedroom, and occasionally the parlor, which was used on special occasions. Even after she grew up Kittie never could use a broom without raising a cloud of dust. And sweeping with an unwieldy broom twice her height without raising the dust would have been a miracle for an eight year old. Her little short, choppy strokes swirled the dust clouds through the air, nearly suffocating her—not to mention gasping Grandma, sitting in her customary rocker by the kitchen window.

Next came the bedroom with its ingrain carpet. This room seemed dustier than the front room, and getting that long broom under the bed was a feat in itself. But to get enough leverage on it to loosen the dirt was an unknown art to Kittie. Hanging on to the dustpan with one hand and on the broom with the other seemed as Herculean a task as cleaning the Stygian stables.

One day while taking a breather Kittie stood taking inventory of the articles on the big, massive bureau. Suddenly her heart turned over before it jumped into her mouth. Her eyes grew large with surprise and fear. And her breath came in quick short gasps. There in plain sight was a human eye staring up at her. She stood riveted to the spot, gazing as one under the influence of hypnotism. She knew that God's eye was always upon her, but whose eye could be watching her from that bureau? She stared at the eye and the eye stared back at her. Had she done a good job sweeping that carpet?

Finally composure again sat upon her young brow and she began work in the big kitchen. With a pan of soapy water it was her duty to wash the wainscoting behind the range and around the corner where Grandma's washstand stood with bottles and pillboxes holding it down.

Grandma was noted for taking medicine. Her philosophy seemed to be "If a little medicine will help, a lot of it will cure." One day she gave curious Kittie a spoonful of something from a bottle. When Kittie reached home, she told her mother that Grandma gave her a spoonful of perfume. "What could it have been?" thought Mother.

Grandpa Lewis was a proverbial chimney—he usually had a corncob pipe in his mouth. He also indulged in chewing tobacco. Behind the stove stood one of those objects that graced the homes and public places in the '90's—a horrid, smelly old spittoon! Sometimes Grandpa aimed too high and his tobacco juice missed the target and went—splat against the wainscoting where it trickled down those numerous cracks and dried. Kittie's efforts with a soapy cloth revived it and it came to life again as strong as when first deposited there. How she hated cleaning that corner! And Grandma's washstand was a miniature drugstore with hair dye and bottles and bottles of the apothecary's mixtures.

The last task completed, Grandma paid Kittie the weekly (or should it be weakly?) sum agreed upon—ten cents. Yes, one whole dime! Kittie deposited it in the little square shiny tin box (a sample pill box) that Grandma had given her for that purpose, and skipped for home—happy and satisfied with her weekly stipend.

Rushing into the house she expected her parents to be as shocked as she was over that terrible eye. Then she learned of Grandpa's accident when he owned a little store in Loretto. Upon opening a keg of nails one day a nail struck him in the eye. Infection set in and he suffered great pain. Surgery became necessary and his eye was removed—the artificial eye replacing it. Seldom was he seen without it. Kittie felt sorry for Grandpa but relieved to know that eye hadn't been watching her.

For once that was one thing that she didn't want—she didn't want to grow up and wear a glass eye! Kittie did, however, watch him and was rewarded by seeing Grandpa putting it under his lid as he held it up. Sometimes she imitated him, pretending that she was putting in her glass eye. She imitated everyone that she saw. The mystery is that she had any individuality of her own.

NOTES

Dust would have been very prevalent in these days because the dirt roads were dusty in dry weather and muddy during wet weather. Paved roadways were unheard of at this time. Also, many floors didn't have carpets or linoleum, as we know it today. Floors might just be hard planks. Floor coverings would have been rugs braided with old rags. Yards would not have been landscaped, as we know them today. Yards might be uneven with tall grass that would be mowed down and used as hay feed for cattle or horses. Sometimes livestock grazed in the yards. Many houses had rail fences around their yards for this purpose. Therefore, it would be very easy to track a considerable amount of dirt and dust into homes.

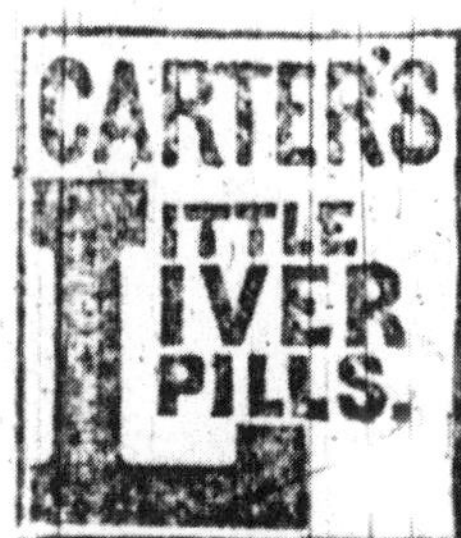

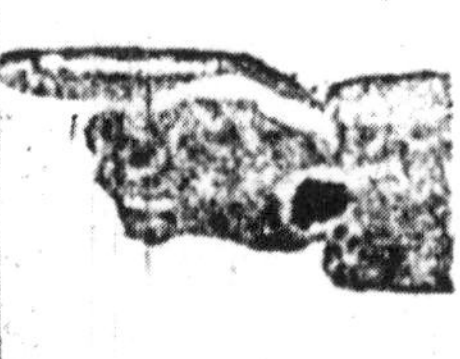

CURE

Sick Headache and relieve all the troubles incident to a bilious state of the system, such as Dizziness, Nausea, Drowsiness, Distress after eating, Pain in the Side, &c. While their most remarkable success has been shown in curing

SICK

Headache, yet Carter's Little Liver Pills are equally valuable in Constipation, curing and preventing this annoying complaint, while they also correct all disorders of the stomach, stimulate the liver and regulate the bowels. Even if they only cured

HEAD

Ache they would be almost priceless to those who suffer from this distressing complaint; but fortunately their goodness does not end here, and those who once try them will find these little pills valuable in so many ways that they will not be willing to do without them. But after all sick head

ACHE

Is the bane of so many lives that here is where we make our great boast. Our pills cure it while others do not.

Carter's Little Liver Pills are very small and very easy to take. One or two pills make a dose. They are strictly vegetable and do not gripe or purge, but by their gentle action please all who use them. In vials at 25 cents; five for $1. Sold by druggists everywhere, or sent by mail.

CARTER MEDICINE CO., New York.

SMALL PILL. SMALL DOSE. SMALL PRICE

2-16swf&wrmly

Most illnesses were treated with patent medicines. Newspapers and magazines were full of patent medicines for all kinds of problems such as those indicated in this 1890s ad. Most people treated themselves with these medicines instead of seeking a physician's care. Carter's Little Liver Pills cured many ailments.
Eddy Historical Collection

Chapter 14

Pins For Sale

Reading material was rather limited. There was *The Toledo Blade,* a weekly newspaper that later became a daily. Mother took two monthly magazines—*Comfort* and *Hearth And Home.* They weren't what we regard as good magazines today with smooth paper, good print, colored illustrations, etc. They were more like the *Saginaw News* Saturday edition of *Radio-TV Guide,* only perhaps smaller and about the thickness of two or three such guides. They contained the usual articles of interest to women: Handwork (knitting, crocheting, quilt making); receipts (recipes, now); stories (good stories, though); ads such as Lydia Pinkham's (a baby in every bottle), Carter's Little Liver Pills, Doane's Kidney Pills, Hair Dye, and the usual free prizes for selling so many articles.

One day came the Ad that a beautiful doll could be had for selling only 20 pins at 10 cents each. What a bargain! Kittie must have that doll! She wanted to try her business acumen, but most of all she wanted that doll!

After anxious days of waiting the box arrived in the mail with 19 celluloid pins and one key ring with a man's chain attached. Good old Uncle Guy was her first customer. "That key ring and chain is just what I've always wanted," he declared. He bought a pin for Aunt Josie. This boosted Kittie's morale and confidence right from the start.

Each pin was attached to a little piece of cardboard, which showed it off beautifully! Saturday morning dawned clear but cold and Gertie and Kittie started off for Aunt Ellen's where Kittie had a vision of seeing all her pins sold.

It was a two and one-half mile walk down the river road (Midland Road) with only five houses along the route—Uncle Herbert, Acker's, Foote's,

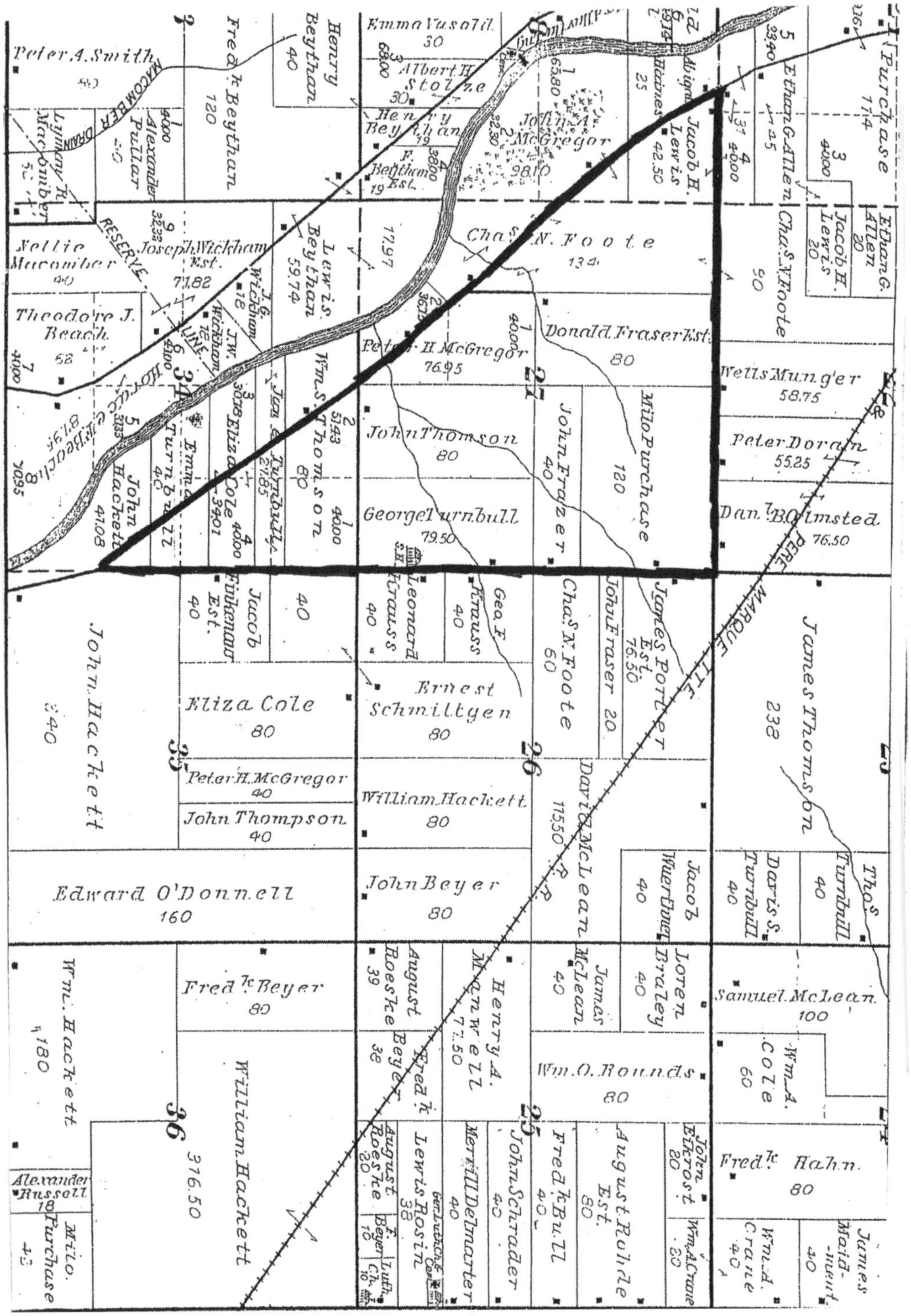

Peter A. Smith
Lyman R. Macomber
Alexander Pullar
Fred. K. Beythan 120
Henry Beythan 40
Emma Vasold 30
Albert H. Stolze
Henry Beythan 19
F. Beythan Est. 19
John A. McGregor 98.10
Abigail Lewis
Jacob H. Lewis 42.50
Purchase 114
Ethan G. Allen 45
Macomber Drain
Nellie Macomber 40
Joseph Wickham Est. 71.82
Reserve Line
Lewis Beythan 59.74
Chas. N. Foote 134
Chas. N. Foote 90
Jacob H. Lewis 20
Ethan G. Allen 20
Theodore J. Beach 62
J. G. Wickham 18
J. W. Wickham 16
Horace C. Beach
Peter H. McGregor 76.95
Donald Fraser Est. 80
Wells Munger 58.75
John Hackett 41.08
Emma Turnbull 40
Eliza Cole 34.01
Jas. G. Turnbull 21.85
Wm. S. Thomson 80
John Thomson 80
John Frazer 40
Milo Purchase 120
Peter Doran 55.25
George Turnbull 79.50
Dan'l B. Olmsted 76.50
Pere Marquette
John Hackett 240
Jacob Finkenaur Est. 40
Leonard Krauss 40
Geo. F. Krauss 40
Chas. N. Foote 60
John Fraser 20
James Porter Est. 76.50
James Thomson 238
Eliza Cole 80
Ernest Schmiltgen 80
Peter H. McGregor 40
John Thompson 40
William Hackett 80
David McLean 115.50
Jacob Wuerfeliner 40
Davis S. Turnbull 40
Thos. Turnbull 40
Edward O'Donnell 160
John Beyer 80
Wm. L. Hackett 180
Fred'k Beyer 80
August Roeske 39
Henry A. Manwell 77.50
James McLean 40
Loren Braley 40
Samuel McLean 100
William Hackett 376.50
August Roeske 38
Fred'k Beyer
Wm. O. Rounds 80
Wm. A. Cole 60
Alexander Russell 18
Milo Purchase
August Roeske 20
Lewis Rosin 38
Merrill DeMarter 40
John Schrader 40
Fred'k Bull 40
August Rohlde Est. 80
John Eikrost 20
Wm. A. Crane 20
Fred'k Hahn 80
Wm. A. Crane 40
James Maidment 40
Ger. Luth. Ch. & Cem.

McGregor's, and Thomson's. Gertie had said she would go but Kittie had to do the talking. A timid knock and a timid voice at each house: "I'm trying to earn a doll. Don't you want to buy a pin? They're only ten cents." And Kittie exhibited the shining beauties! Whether it was her diminutive size, her apparent fear, or the craving to own one of those flashy bargains she reached Aunt Ellen's house five pins less and 50 cents in her purse.

At the last stop Mrs. Thomson, a rather spicy, crusty sort of person, had invited them in to get warm and had treated them to hot fried cakes, fresh from the piping hot kettle. Her kindness and the fried cakes really warmed the cockles of their hearts. They reached Aunt Ellen's before noon and had dinner there. Then the sales talk again. Aunt Pollie bought a deep pink—almost cerise celluloid flower pin. But Aunt Ellen looked them over and said she would buy one if there was a black one (which there wasn't, of course). Imagine Kittie's horror of a black flower!

Too much like a mourning veil! Aunt Ellen was still wearing mourning for Uncle John and in those days mourning meant *BLACK*. Uncle John had been a prosperous farmer and lumberman and was considered quite wealthy, but Aunt Ellen couldn't humor her little niece by buying for ten cents something that she couldn't wear. She could have bought several and given them to the girls. But in those days her mind was so preoccupied with her own troubles. Kittie couldn't understand that in the face of all those pretty pins.

Well, that meant a longer walk home because they would have to go up Garfield Road two miles and then one and one-half miles west on Pierce Road. This took them past eight more houses: Myers', Fraser's, Krause's, Porter's, Purchase's, Olmsted's, Doran's, and Munger's (Albert's mother). The day was a regular Horatio Alger success story, and two little girls arrived home at the end of the day—weary and hungry, but happy—only a few pins short of owning the coveted prize doll!

Facing Page:
This partial 1896 map shows the long walk the girls took to sell their pins. They would have left their home nearby Pierce Road, walked down Midland Road to John Hackett, then returned home on the Garfield Road, passing the Porter Schoolhouse, walking up to Pierce Road, turning west on Pierce and then back home. At least a seven-mile walk! Their route is outlined in a heavy black line. Vasold Collection

Eventually the pins were sold and the $2 dispatched through the mail. At last the Red Letter Day came announcing that the new doll was at the railroad station. But there was a string attached—in the form of 90 cents express charges! Nearly a day's wages and the doll wasn't worth that much! But Father couldn't disappoint Kittie after all her effort and faith, so the freight charges were paid and the doll and her new mother were together at last after she was freed from the excelsior in which she had been packed. It was a blue eyed, yellow haired doll much smaller than her nice doll, Kathleen. The wooden body was topped with a bisque head. Like any new mother Kittie thought her child beautiful.

One night Kittie forgot and left her doll in a hammock that she had contrived from an old horse fly net. A rain during the night dissolved the connective tissue in the doll's joints. Her head came off and the arms and legs were severed. An anatomy of disconnected members and a memory were all that remained of the hard-earned Mail Order Doll. Kittie's first and last business venture! And a motto to live by: "Never leave a prized possession outdoors in the rain."

NOTES

Kittie and Gertie would have started out from their house just south of Pierce Road and walked down Midland Road past the first five houses to reach her Aunt Ellen Hackett's farmhouse. John Hackett owned a large parcel of land next to Tittabawassee Road and the Tittabawassee River on both sides of Midland Road. He was considered quite wealthy in these days.

John Hackett was born on October 24, 1830 in New York. He was one of the five children of Bernard and Bridget Hackett who had come to Tittabawassee Township in 1843. His marriage to Ellen Allen produced one son, John Thomas Hackett, born November 22, 1874 and died May 25, 1907. John Hackett died on June 22, 1901. Aunt Ellen Hackett was mourning her husband's 1901 death during the girls' visit to her. Ellen eventually sold the Freeland property and she and Pollie moved to Saginaw.

The other four children of Bernard Hackett were Christopher born 1823, Catherine born 1833, Thomas born 1831 and who married Jesse McGregor, and William born 1843 who married Mary McKeller. Early maps also show William Hackett as a large landowner nearby John Hackett's farms.

Several of the people mentioned in this chapter would have been related to each other.

On their return trip the girls would have walked up to Garfield Road, past the Porter School, turning west on Pierce Road, past the eight houses mentioned, before returning to their own home on the southeast corner of Pierce and Midland Roads. Altogether the little girls would have walked almost seven miles that day to sell their pins!

Farm Res. of WILLIAM HACKETT
Sec. 36, Tittabawassee Tp. Saginaw Co. Mich.

As shown on the above illustration, William Hackett also was a large, wealthy landowner. He and John Hackett were brothers. Both were sons of Bernard Hackett who had settled in the township in 1843. This sketch of William's farm is from the 1877 Atlas and indicates a large farming operation with several buildings, roaming cattle, and large fenced-in fields. John's farm would be similar to William's. Vasold Collection

Chapter 15

The Test of a Gentleman

Louise and Kittie decided it was time for them to do their haying. Kittie went to the pantry and got two pieces of molasses cake. The two girls squeezed and squeezed the cake, pressing it into hard plugs of tobacco! This they carried in the back pocket of their imaginary overalls. (In reality their apron pockets.) They'd take out the plug now and then, biting off a chew. And after chewing awhile they would spit the yellow juice out as they'd seen men do. And then they would wipe their hot faces with their big red bandanna handkerchiefs (imaginary ones, of course).

Off they went walking east down on the narrow dirt Pierce Road toward the field. They were gathering little wisps of hay here and there that had been overlooked or had dropped from the big hay wagon.

Quite some distance away Mr. Jack Doran was coming west on the same road with a team and heavy binder. Kittie conceived a very bright idea. "Let's stay in the road and keep right on going," she said. "If he's a gentleman, he'll turn out for us because we're ladies." On they went and on he came, putting less distance between them at every step. It became clear that Jack's idea of what constitutes a lady or a gentleman didn't coincide with theirs.

When they got close enough to see the whites of his eyes and could almost feel the hot air from the horses' nostrils, the girls stopped and Jack did too. He gave them a withering look, which made their backbones bristle, but they stood adamant as the Rock of Gibraltar.

Jack weighed 225 pounds or more and they knew if he wanted to he could make mincemeat of them. The girls almost expected to hear him boom out in a giant voice: "Fee, Fi, Fo, Fum, I smell the blood of an Englishman!" But instead, he roared like an angry bull, "You #!! d---little fools #!!, get out of the way! Don't you know any better than to hold up a team of horses with a binder?" Kittie's bristles developed goose pimples and she said. "I guess we'd better get out of his way but anyway—he's no gentleman!" The starch had gone out of her backbone.

Another remark from him calling them #!! d---little fools #!! and the interested parties went on their way, Jack boiling under the collar and the little girls as angry as a couple of young roosters sparring at each other.

Jack was a rough appearing man but he told his sister (later Aunt Annie) about the incident, laughing at the way two #!! d---little fools #!! had defied him. A few days later he left some paper dolls and a homely mask at the house because "I heard that the girls like to play tramp." (Lucky for Kittie that he didn't make any other explanation.) He had done this more out of admiration for her spunk than from any compunction of his conscience.

For some unknown reason Kittie kept this episode a secret from her parents until many years later. Her mother said it was lucky for her that she hadn't told it. But to give credit where it is due she didn't do that to be smart or mean. She was looking at the whole affair from a child's viewpoint. She was familiar with the principle—the proper treatment of a lady by a gentleman. But the application of the principle was something her little independent mind didn't understand so well. Next time she'd choose her gentleman!

NOTES

Chapter 11 explains how Kittie used the homely mask from Jack Doran when she played tramp and teased cousin Louise. Jack Doran lived on the Doran farm on Pierce Road a short distance east of the Lewis' farms. They would have been rural neighbors within one mile of each other.

CHAPTER 16

THE FAMILY ADDITION

At last the awaited addition to the family arrived. Chubby and plump, it seemed as though he was as broad as he was long. His long, silky brown hair, soft brown eyes (something new in the Lewis family—all the others had blue) and his endearing way won a big warm spot in the heart of each member of the family.

Mother had the privilege of naming this baby as she had promised herself a few years back. Why she decided upon the name she did was a mystery. Perhaps she hadn't had enough experience in naming her babies. We felt sure she wasn't thinking of that cruel Roman emperor when she named him Nero. At any rate Nero was the name given to their new baby, a six-week-old Shepherd puppy—one from a litter belonging to our southern neighbors, the Ackers.

Murl Freeland and Louise were there when he arrived—the cutest, youngest puppy they had ever seen.

Father had built a big porch on the back of the house—or rather the floor of their future new kitchen. It was flat like a table and Nero was put up there while the girls stood on the ground guarding him to see that he didn't fall off. The worshipful affection of four girls was lavished upon him, and he was so roly-poly and cunning that he sent them in gales of laughter.

When night came Nero was so lonesome for the other puppies in the litter that he whooped her up for a "fare you well." The next night the folks were entertaining the new minister, Reverend Allene. He was either a candidate or had been hired and had come on ahead of his family. Since he was to stay overnight the folks thought it would be a good time for him to meet the young folks of the church.

Father had laid a new floor in the attic, and it would make an ideal place for the young folks to play *Snap And Catch 'Em, We've Got A New Pig In The Parlor,* and other games of the '90's. *Catch And Kiss 'Em* would seem a better name for that was the object of the game. A small group huddled together, a young lady ran around the group, and if the pursuing young man caught her he kissed her. Several groups could be playing at the same time in a large room, giving more girls the thrill of being kissed! What a game! Floyd's crowd always played this game, and all her young life Kittie looked forward to the time when she could play it—and Post Office, too. But before that day had arrived these games had been discarded giving place to *Happy Is The Miller, Three Deep, The Virginia Reel,* and *Wink 'Em.* Kittie always thought she was born thirty years either too soon or too late!

Murl came down during the day so as to be there early. The Reverend also arrived. But that evening a terrible electric storm came. The night was pitch black, the rain came in torrents, the lightning literally split the sky and the thunder rolled and cracked making a deafening noise. The dirt roads quickly became muddy, and the inky blackness made travel impossible at a time when most of the folks from Freeland would have to walk with no lights to light the way. Kerosene lamps were the order of the day then. No one could get there. Reverend Allene was the whole party.

Mother knew that Nero would whimper and cry and howl all night, keeping the Reverend awake. But what to do with him? He couldn't be left outdoors, and all the barns were across the road on Grandpa's farm. All but the outhouse!

Ah! She'd put Nero out there and get him out in the morning before the Reverend had to take his constitutional. This building was known by several names—back house, toilet, privy, and Mrs. Jones' house—and, if one wanted to be vulgar—it was known by another name. Regardless of which name you called it, it smelled the same!

Nero was stowed away out there after everyone had made the customary before-bedtime visit. Early next morning Mother went out to get Nero—and lo and behold—he wasn't there! But hearing a moaning, whimpering cry coming from down under a hole—the most forlorn, bedraggled puppy in all creation

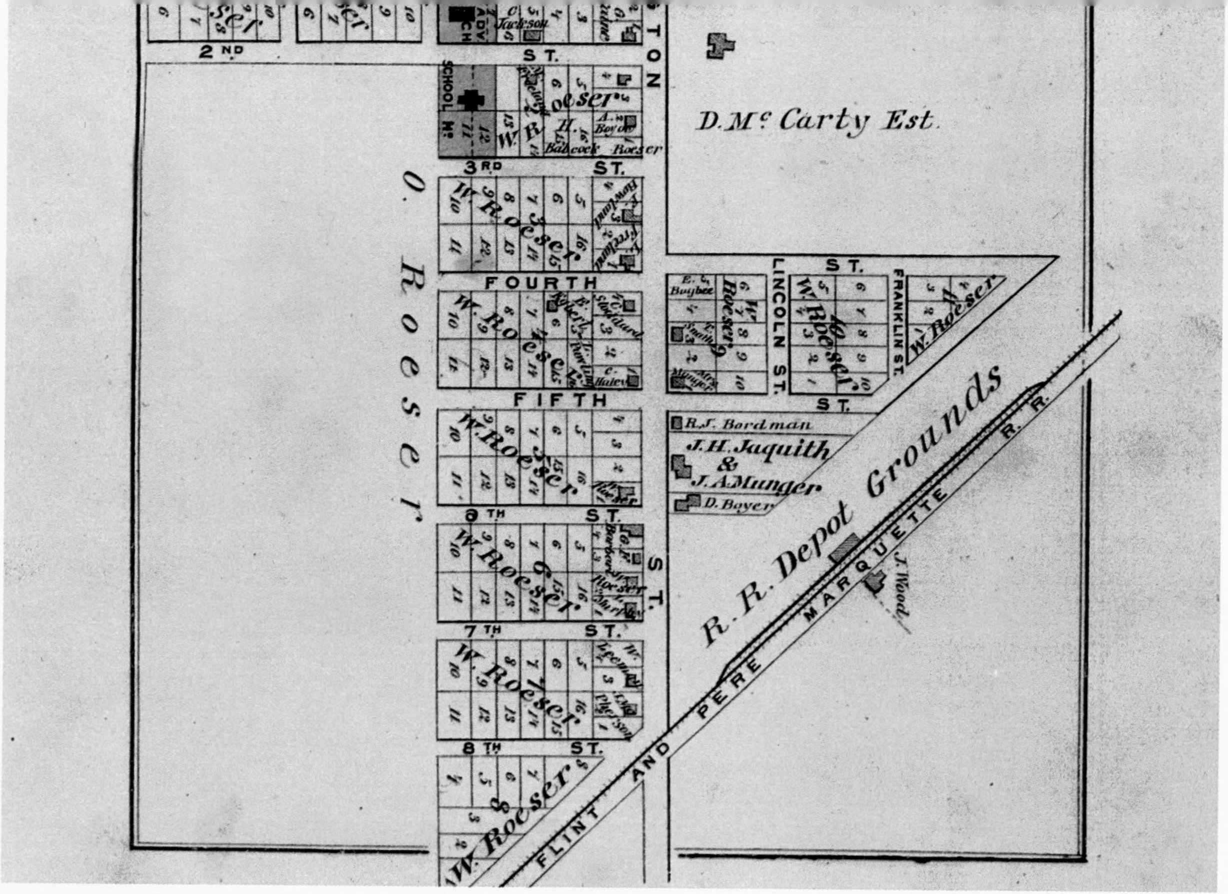

2ND
ST.
SCHOOL No.
3RD ST.
FOURTH
FIFTH
6TH ST.
7TH ST.
8TH ST.
O. Roeser
W. Roeser
W. R. H. Roeser
D. McCarty Est.
LINCOLN ST.
FRANKLIN ST.
R.J. Bordman
J.H. Jaquith & J.A. Munger
D. Boyer
R. R. Depot Grounds
FLINT AND PERE MARQUETTE R. R.
J. Wood

Taken from 1877 Atlas

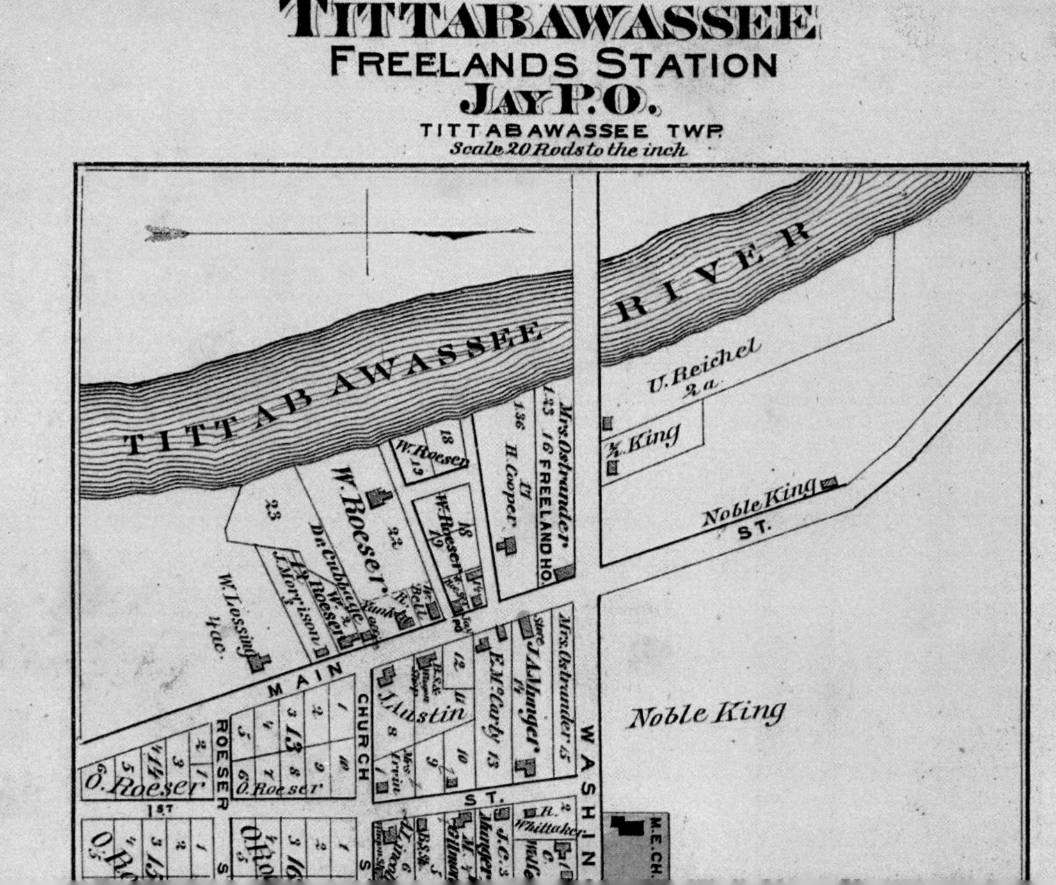
TITTABAWASSEE
FREELANDS STATION
JAY P.O.
TITTABAWASSEE TWP.
Scale 20 Rods to the inch
TITTABAWASSEE RIVER
U. Reichel
King
Noble King
ST.
Noble King
Mrs. Ostrander
FREELAND HO.
H. Cooper
W. Roeser
W. Roeser
Dr. Cubbage
J. Morrison
W. Lossing
MAIN
CHURCH
ROESER
1ST
O. Roeser
O. Roeser
J. Austin
E. McCarty
J. A. Munger
Mrs. Ostrander
WASHIN
ST.
R. Whittaker
M.E.CH.

looked pitifully up at her. It never was figured out how Nero succeeded in getting up on that seat.

By the time the children and the Reverend were astir, Nero had had his first soapy bath and was reposing in a dry towel in front of the kitchen stove.

Father was always a deacon and trustee in the church and arrangements always had to be made for them when new ministers came candidating. Mother was generally stuck with them! They hadn't expected the puppy until a few days later when arrangements had been made for the Reverend. Mother surely won Nero's good will, affection, and loyalty through her Good Samaritan act.

Nero was the smartest dog the family ever had. He could roll over, shake hands, walk on his hind legs, speak, jump rope, and do any trick they tried to teach him. He was a useful dog on the farm: driving cows to pasture; chasing hens from the garden; chasing strange farm animals that strayed there; and was a good watch dog. When Uncle Guy needed him he would whistle or call him, and Nero went bounding over there on the run. But when he was through, he went home immediately.

One day Mother was away and came home rather late. Looking through the dining room window she stood outside laughing at the funny sight she saw. Nero was sitting on a chair at the supper table with the family. Floyd was putting Karo corn syrup on top of Nero's nose, and he was nearly pulling his tongue from its roots as he reached it up and tried to lick every vestige of syrup.

As soon as he licked it clean, Floyd would put another daub there. Nero sat licking and drooling, the saliva running from the sides of his mouth in a steady flow—equal in output to that of Niagara Falls.

On school days Nero would begin looking at the clock and then at Mother about 3:30 o'clock. A little after 4 o'clock she'd let him out and he'd go and sit at the top of Uncle Guy's hill, watching up the road. When the girls came in sight off he'd bound! Then he'd carry their lunch box home, his head held high and his plumy tail wagging happily. Mother always gave him the leftovers from the lunch box, and the girls always saw there were some leftovers. He was the idol of the family and should have been called Prince or King.

One night Nero's brother came along from Acker's and the two playful dogs ran off together. When he didn't appear in the morning Father was suspicious of the two shots he had heard early in the morning. The dogs had run across Charles Thomson's farm and he said they were chasing sheep (a story the family discounted). At any rate the dogs met their tragic fate that night. It was a time of mourning at the Lewis house. No one could talk about it. The whole neighborhood grieved over it. It made strained relations with Mr. Thomson for some time. Every time the girls and Louise walked past his home on the way to school their eyes would squint, their muscles became taut, and they swore vengeance—though they didn't know what form it would take. On the way home from school in a grassy ditch by Thomson's pigpen they discovered a nestful of hens' eggs. What a find! Shaking them they knew they were rotten. Better yet! The time for putting vengeance into effect had come.

One by one the girls hurled these eggs against a granary near the road. The brittle shells broke easily spilling the greasy, smelly, yellow contents down the clapboard side of the building. Every time an egg hit its target the girls swelled with satisfaction.

When the last egg had trickled its odorous contents down the side, the girls had vented their spleen—vengeance had taken its toll—and a healthier atmosphere had been created. But those greasy streaks remained on the building for years. No amount of rain could wash them off—water and oil won't mix! Those streaks were as difficult to remove as the d---spot that Lady Mac Beth tried to rub out.

Nero's loyal slaves had had their vengeance, as those greasy streaks testified. But that didn't bring Nero back. Two beautiful dogs had been sacrificed by a poor sportsman, but the whole neighborhood was richer for having known them.

NOTES

Since the girls walked north on Main Street to their school, Charles Thomson's farm must also have been north of their home on Main Street also known as Midland Road today. According to Chapter 18 the Thomsons and Purchases lived together in the Purchase house on the Purchase farm. Early maps show Harriet Purchase or O.R. Purchase as the owner.

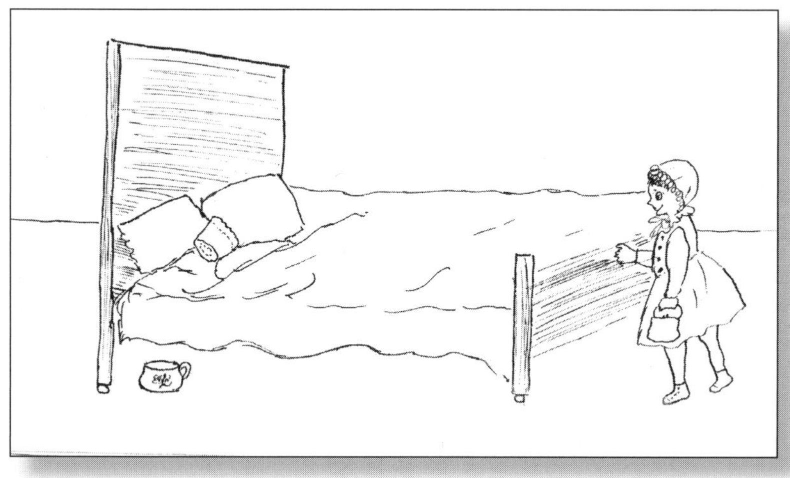

Chapter 17

Disillusion

Ever since she could remember Kittie had been a great lover of babies. If she saw a baby anywhere she didn't know anything else. From the time she was five years old, Kittie began coaxing her mother to get a baby. She thought it would be so nice for her mother to have a baby of her own.

Julia Clark, a schoolmate of the same age, said one day, "You look like your mother." This pleased Kittie but she remembered the maxim—"Honesty is the best policy," so she told Julia, "She isn't really my mother. I really belong to old Mrs. Emery. She gave me to my mother. I'm glad because I wouldn't want to live with her—she looks so cross." Julia said, "Why, I never knew that!" Neither did anyone else!

Kittie continued, "We don't any of us belong to Mother. Floyd belongs to old Mrs. Doran and Gertie belongs to Mrs. Johnson." Well, the way Julia took all this news made Kittie feel pretty important—sort of set apart from others. She and her brother and sister were all made of different clay, and yet by hook or crook had all happened to get into the same family with the best Father and Mother in the world. At least they hadn't been found under cabbage plants the way some babies had been! Every time she looked at big, cross-looking Mrs. Emery at church Kittie used to send up a little prayer of thanksgiving that she had given her to Father and Mother.

Fate had been kind to her and Floyd especially. Gertie's real mother was pretty and nice, but not as nice as Mother.

After coaxing so long for a baby her mother said, "Well, maybe when you get home from school some day you'll find a baby on the bed." Like the eagle Kittie's hopes began to soar. Each night when reaching home she'd tiptoe in and look on Mother's bed.

Kittie wanted a baby just like this one! But she had to wait until her beloved little niece, Virginia Claire Olmsted, was born December 1, 1912. This is Virginia in 1913.

Mother grew tired of this so she said to herself, "I'll cure her of this." She rolled up a bundle, putting a shawl around it and a little bonnet on its head. Then turning its "face" to the wall and covering it with a blanket, she awaited the result.

The usual procedure! Kittie looked and there on the bed was their baby! A little baby brother! Expectation had finally ripened into fulfillment. Reaching over to touch it she received the jolt of a lifetime. "That isn't a baby—that's just a make-believe baby! Just a bundle of clothes!" Different emotions surged through her breast—surprise, wonder, and disappointment. Her dream of a baby had vanished in thin air like a rainbow-colored soap bubble—leaving just a semblance of a reminder to show it had been there. Thus ended the expectation of any more babies in their family.

In later years Mother told her she grew tired of having her ask for and look for a baby—it was annoying to her sometimes when company was there so she thought she would cure her once for all. She did! But she felt very sorry and ashamed when she saw Kittie's ecstasy followed by disappointment and disillusionment. And Mother had to go through life mothering three children that she never really "borned!"

Chapter 18

Scavenger Hunts

They weren't called that then. They were more on the order of snooping. A vacant house, a trash can, or a junk pile is always a source of fascination to a child. And the girls were no exception to the rule. Even a backhouse figured in their many treasure hunts.

The Jack Purchase Family had the nicest-looking outhouse the girls had seen. It was almost square made of nice lumber, and had a four-sided roof instead of the traditional two-sided one meeting at the ridge. It had a little cupola where the four sides met on the roof. But the exterior of that building wasn't the attraction. Oh, no!

Necessity had called to one of the girls one night on the way home from school. And having seen the interior, they felt impelled to stop occasionally if not regularly. In a box fastened to the northeast corner walls were magazines and catalogs with COLORED pictures—a thing unheard of, especially in a backhouse. Most of the pictures in their books and magazines were black and white—mostly black.

As they turned the pages a lovely vision met their gaze. Beautiful ladies dressed in the height of fashion in bright blues, reds, greens, and every color of the rainbow. What a wonderful source for a box of paper dolls—and free! They were printed on glossy, shiny paper so what were they doing in a backhouse? Newspapers could do just as well there! And there were cute babies, dolls, flowers, and a variety of pictures that would be exquisite decorations on homemade valentines!

They didn't exactly think of it as stealing, and yet they wanted to carry them away unseen. With one girl standing guard at a crack in the doorway, the others ripped the precious pages from the coveted catalogs and tucked them inside their coats or dresses. With the guard's announcement that all was clear all three crept cautiously forth, with guilt-laden faces but hearts full of joy. They put on speed for a few rods and then slowed down when it became evident they weren't being pursued.

Thereafter, whenever they wanted more colored pictures they knew exactly where to find them. If the Purchases or Thomsons who lived together in that large brick house (Phettaplace) saw the girls surreptitiously entering and leaving Mrs. Jones' house so often, they must have wondered why they couldn't make a ten or fifteen minute walk from school without requiring the services of a halfway house. Years later Kittie told Mrs. Phettaplace (Purchase's daughter) about the stolen treasures and she nearly laughed her head off.

Just south of the Purchase house was the vacant old Hilton house, which stood at the top of the hill above the river. Like any vacant house it was waiting to be explored. At the back of the house was an old dilapidated porch, high above the ground—and underneath, an open cistern with no cover and nearly full of water. Crawling under that cobwebby porch and peering into that cistern became routine to the three tomboys. Goose pimples raced up and down their backbones as they envisioned what it would mean to slip into that murky water. But the danger element made it more adventurous and attractive. Their guardian angels must have hovered closely over them for they always crawled away safely.

Rummaging in that same house one night Kittie let out a cry of ecstasy. There in a pile of rubbish lay an old music book that must have come from the Ark. But to her it symbolized a musical career for her. It had stiff board covers, buck wheat notes and yellowed pages. But no queen was ever more proud of her scepter and crown than was Kittie as she walked away hugging that music book.

All the way home she walked on a cloud of music. Racing breathlessly into the house she exclaimed, "Now I can take music lessons—here's my music book."

Father and Mother knew that it takes more than a music book, and they weren't sure they could spare the necessary where-with-all that would have to be planked down with every lesson. But reluctant about dampening her ardor, they agreed to talk it over. Kittie knew her parents well enough to know that when they said that it was as good as in the bag. Already she could see herself the Church Organist!

Knowing her love of music, her strong sense of rhythm and her burning desire to play her parents finally said, "If you are willing to practice an hour each day, and will always play when anyone asks you to without being coaxed, we'll see that you have lessons." So many musicians at that time when asked to play would make excuses and say, "Oh, I can't play without my music." If they had asked Kittie to forfeit her eyeteeth in the bargain, she would have done it. Those promises were readily given—and kept, in spite of her craze for tomboyish play.

But needless to say—her lessons were never given from that old book. The first thing her teacher required was a *Kohler's Book for Beginners.* But the book had been the opening wedge!

Out behind Aunt Ellen's farmhouse was a junk pile. Every summer Gertie and Kittie visited their Aunts Ellen and Pollie for two days and nights. Before ending their visit a search was made of that rubbish. One day a ribbed glass lamp with a handle minus a chimney, but otherwise intact, was brought to light from the debris. A chimney would be easy to get. Now they could have a lamp of their own in their bedroom, and they used this lamp for years, as it was easy to carry from place to place.

Louise and Kittie were playing circus along the road across from Louise's house. They couldn't resist a pile of broken bottles, dishes, etc. along the old board fence. Reaching into it to pluck a treasure Kittie cut the middle finger on her right hand, and the blood trickled down her finger. This gave her the idea of being a clown in the circus. So making funny faces at an imaginary audience she walked along with long strides, waving a bloody finger at them. As the finger stopped bleeding and the blood dried on she forgot about the cut and they turned from circus to other play. When it came to play the girls were always versatile.

About two weeks later at school Kittie's finger began to pain, throbbing with every heartbeat. She could hardly bear the pain when she put her hand on her lap. So most of the day she sat with her palm up, her finger sticking up in the air. That seemed to slow down the throbbing process. She was too timid to mention it to her teacher. Teachers were hired to train the mind—the home was to take care of the body!

A large bunch showed up on the little finger side of her wrist. It was a red, ugly looking thing. At home she told about the cut finger, which had been forgotten at the time. A trip was made to Dr. Cubbage's office. He pronounced it blood poisoning and said it would have to be lanced. She didn't know what that meant but it sounded ominous.

Father took her on his knee (no, not turned over it); the doctor brought an odd looking sharp little knife which he sterilized. And sitting down in front of Father's knees, he plunged it into the inflamed wrist. Kittie had turned her face away from him and sat looking at her father. As she felt the knife go in, she winced and made a wry face but was plucky enough not to cry or say anything. A quantity of yellow pus emerged; some smelly medicine was used on it; and a neat gauze dressing was held in place by a gauze bandage.

Good old Dr. Cubbage, who had attended her in her numerous illnesses and upon whom she looked as her second father, patted her hand and said she was his brave little girl.

Father drove to Dietiker's store and bought her a bag of candy of her own choosing—a sort of white taffy drops with pink and brown swirls in them. They really were delectable. Kittie felt like a heroine in a book with all the attention that bandaged wrist brought her at home and at school.

There were other treasure hunts; but no treasures more rewarding than the colored fashion plates, the murky open cistern, the antiquated music book, the lamp (even though it wasn't Aladdin's), and the treacherous broken bottle!

NOTES

The Purchase property and Hilton property with its Hilton Hotel had been part of the original Loretto community. Just northeast of Pierce Road was Jacob H. Lewis' farm, with Josephine Allen's farm, which had originally been Jefferson Jaquith's farm, next to it. North of the Allen farm was the Hilton farm and then the Purchase farm north of that.

The girls would have had to walk past both the Purchase and Hilton property before reaching their homes.

Kittie apparently learned her music well because she was the organist and pianist for the Congregational Church for fifty years.

Aunt Ellen was married to John Hackett and their property was south of Pierce Road next to the Tittabawassee River and Tittabawassee Road, about a two-mile walk from the Lewis farm. A description of the farm is given in Chapters 14 and 23.

Dr. Cline's house and dentist's office on Washington Street, north of Howd's Store on Depot Street, is the first house by the white fence. Wood is piled by the side of the house. An outhouse is next to another shed in the back yard. The railroad track runs in front of the house. The street is muddy and unpaved. Vasold Collection

CHAPTER 19

DR. CLINE, DENTIST

The slogan, "Visit your dentist twice a year," hadn't become standard procedure in the '90's. Children were to memorize such important physiological facts as: There are 208 bones in the body; two kinds of muscles—voluntary and involuntary; the heart beats 72 times per minute (whether one is sleeping or experiencing the exhilaration of a merry-go-round ride); the fingers and toes are called phalanges; the brain has three parts—cerebrum, cerebellum, and medulla oblongata; a better name for belly is abdomen; and a hundred and more important interesting facts about the human body. Children ate up those facts as avidly as a hen takes to water. They were very unfortunate—they hadn't yet discovered that "Crest prevents tooth decay."

So their incisors and molars weren't very well protected. This often led to that ache of all aches—toothache! The ache that made one feel that her mouth was full of demons, each one sticking a needle into her jaw—and each one trying to get his jab in first. Many a night the girls cried themselves to sleep with a toothache.

One morning when Kittie could stand it no longer, her mother gave her 25 or 50 cents and she was to go after school to Dr. Cline, the local dentist who knew as much about extracting teeth as a babe knows about astronauts. All day she looked forward to this with trepidation.

After school Kittie and Louise went to the east end of town where Dr. Cline had a little office north of Howd's Store on Depot Street. The Doctor was a cadaverous looking man with snapping black eyes, black hair, a gruff voice and a very heavy black mustache (the pride of his life), which he kept twirled high toward his ears. His office equipment consisted principally of a dentist's chair, a shelf with some forceps, and a sort of spittoon (waterworks hadn't been installed in that day).

As Kittie got up into the chair and the doctor fastened a towel across her chest, she told him in a timid voice: "Ma said for you to use some cocaine." Thereupon he handed her a little bottle and told her to rub some on. He didn't say where to rub it so she rubbed a generous supply on the tooth instead of on the gum. In later years she discovered it had to be injected into the gum to be effective.

Dr. Cline took up the forceps and said, "Open your mouth." She obliged him but he growled, "Open wider!" She opened wider and thinking the top of her head might come off if she opened any wider he said, "That's good. That'll do." He got a good firm grip on that aching molar and it felt as though he were trying to twist it out of the tender gum. (Goom we used to call it.) As the forceps really grabbed hold Kittie began to rise up off that chair and starting on middle "C" she yelled "*OH*!" Going up to "E" she let out a louder "*OH*!" and the final "*OH*" ended on "G" and the next thing she saw was that cussed tooth hanging to his forceps in front of her.

Louise stood there and listening to the various pitched *OH's* must have thought it was a Prima Donna warming up her voice preparatory to singing her role in *Faust* or *Aida.*

The tooth out, Dr. Cline handed her a glass of water and told her to rinse out her mouth. Kittie took a big mouthful and swished it back and forth. Puffing out first one cheek and then the other as the water was propelled from one side to the other with a gurgling sound. After much swishing and gurgling and spitting she paid her fee and came away from her first and last and only visit to Dr. Cline, Dentist. At any rate Kittie was able to sleep that night.

The summer Floyd died (1959) he was here one Sunday and described his experience with the same dentist. He said the doctor kept letting his forceps slip off the tooth—which is as painful as the extraction. Soon he broke off a piece and it ached worse than ever, as the nerve was more exposed. After several attempts the doctor said he wasn't going to be able to pull it. "Well, you are going to pull it!" said Floyd. "I can't go with it broken this way." And he declared that the doctor finally had him down on the floor, his knee upon his chest and at long last he finally extracted the stubborn tooth. Floyd's nerves

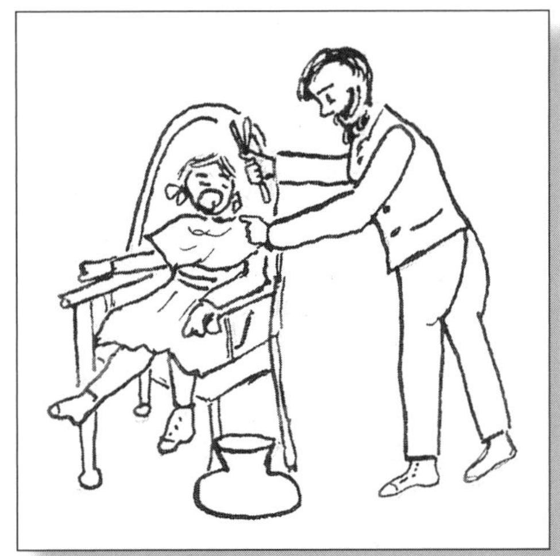

had about reached the limit and the dentist's temper was just going above boiling point. Whether quite all the details were true, Kittie could not say, but Floyd gave the impression that it all happened that way. But Kittie did know that his work was murderous! Kittie could swear he was a blinger of a dentist. He should have changed his sign to read: "Dr. Cline, Butcher."

Too bad they hadn't had Anacin that three out of four doctors recommend for "fast, fast, fast relief." Wonder what that fourth doctor recommends—perhaps "Bengay that rubs pain away." Excuse the slide. Must be pain on the downgrade!

One time Gertie had been having the toothache. I think it was one of her temporary teeth. Father persuaded her to let him tie a string to it and the other end of the string to the doorknob. He told her to keep looking in the pail of water that he had set in front of her. She followed his directions meticulously. He threw a bar of soap or something into the pail splashing the water into her face. He expected it would startle her enough to make her jump, thus pulling the tooth. But she just stood and stared into that pail as mooly as a cow stares one in the face without blinking. Father laughed and said, "Why didn't you jump?" "Well," she said, "If I had, my tooth would have come out." That was once when Father's plans were abortive.

NOTES

Dr. Cline's office was at the far east end of the Freeland Village, near the Pere Marquette Railroad tracks. When Kittie got out of school, she would have walked north on Second Street to Washington Street and then continued east for five blocks until reaching Dr. Cline's office.

Chapter 20

Home Remedies for the Ailing

More sleepless nights! Earache! As Amos always says, "If it isn't one thing it's the same thing." This isn't quite the same thing as the toothache because in addition to the stabbing pain it has a crackety, crackety crack feeling as though the hammer, anvil, and stirrup bones are all striking the nerve instead of each other.

The aggravating pain drove sleep from the house. As Kittie's lusty howls filled the night air Mother heated sweet oil and put a few drops in her ear, plugging it with a wad of cotton. If that didn't help Father got up and lighted up—smoking in her ear.

The warm tobacco fumes laden with nicotine got in their best licks after awhile, and the pain subsided enough to let the household get some shut-eye. And Father had had a few extra puffs of his favorite brand tobacco!

When nothing worked then a few drops of paregoric in water taken internally sometimes did the trick. Kittie loved paregoric—it tasted a little like licorice candy! She was mighty thankful she didn't have to go to Dr. Cline and have her ears pulled. What a boon Sleep-eze is to sufferers today—Sleep-eze with no drug hangover and no drug habit! In her later life Kittie thought she was born 60 instead of 30 years too soon.

Floyd and Gertie were subject to Quinzy, a very painful throat infection. They had it almost every winter. All three children had tonsillitis now and then. For these two infections Dr. Cubbage usually prescribed.

The standard remedy for simple sore throat was a gargle of paregoric and water or, more available and probably more effective—salt and water.

Sometimes dry sulphur was plastered on the tonsils, and some more sulphur was sprinkled on the hot lid of the cook stove. Kittie loved this treatment because she loved sulphur, and because the sulphur burned blue—a purple blue like fireworks as she bent over the stove inhaling the fumes which smarted the eyes and throat but seemed to reach the infected area.

Then if the sulphur treatment failed a slice of fat raw pork (always available) with a generous sprinkling of black pepper on it was wrapped around the throat at bedtime, and a stocking wrapped around over this fat, peppery application. The pork and pepper were expected to draw the poison from the throat—right through the neck, apparently. Unlike Ben-Gay—it was not greaseless. By morning the neck had a greasy, blotchy red appearance and if the sore throat was not better good old Dr. Cubbage was called.

One day during a school session a big boy, Ray Denison, asked Kittie if she liked white sulphur. "I don't know—I've never tasted white sulphur but I like yellow sulphur," she said. "How nice of him!" she thought. He handed her a generous helping but it proved to be quinine and her estimate of Ray went down to zero as she had a bitter mouthful and no place to spit. That was once she had the urge to kill!

Sweet Quinine

IS A RECENT IMPROVEMENT

Replaces the use of the BITTER SULPHATE QUININE, with which all are familiar.

Dose for dose, it is

WARRANTED

FULLY EQUAL IN EVERY WAY TO BITTER QUININE,

AND LIKE IT IS THE ONE

GREAT, POSITIVE and UNFAILING

CURE

FOR all DISEASES of MALARIOUS ORIGIN.

Fever and Ague,
Intermittent Fever,
Chill Fever,
Remittent Fever,
Bilious Fever,
Dumb Ague,

and the long train of disorders following these when neglected.

SWEET QUININE

is made solely from Peruvian Bark, (so is *Bitter Quinine*,) therefore is of Vegetable origin, and not a Mineral poison, but on the contrary is proved to be one of the elements found in the blood of all healthy persons.

SWEET QUININE

acts as an antidote to, (as well as a cure for,) malarial or miasmatic poison, the absorption of which by the lungs causes Intermittent Fevers, etc. The only advantage claimed for

SWEET QUININE

over the use of old Bitter Quinine, is the entire absence of that intense, persistent bitterness, which in the latter is an insurmountable obstacle to its use with most persons and always with children.

SWEET QUININE

is in two forms—in Powder for the use of Physicians and Druggists, and Fluid, for use in the family and for the general public.

Stearns, Farr & Co.

MANUFACTURING CHEMISTS,

NEW YORK.

Quinine was the standard medicine for all illnesses and was easily obtainable, as noted in this 1870 newspaper advertisement.
Eddy Historical Collection

More than half a century later what a fortune the Dow Chemical Company

has made from basic sulphur and brine! So the good old sulphur, yellow or white, had its therapeutic value at the time.

Then as now colds were always in circulation. Father's remedy for that: Soak the feet in water as hot as you could stand; drink a cup of piping hot ginger tea (the ginger making it doubly hot); and go to bed, sweating out your cold while you slept.

In addition to this heat treatment hot turpentine and lard were rubbed on the chest, and covered with a piece of flannel pinned inside the outing flannel nightgown. If the cold was on the lungs the doctor ordered a mustard plaster made of one part of dry mustard and two parts of flour mixed with enough water to make a paste. Then this was spread on a cloth and put in a homemade cloth bag and placed on the chest. This made the chest almost as red as a peony. In addition there was Father's old standby—quinine. Father would buy a bottle of quinine and fill the empty capsules himself.

One was never quite certain which remedy had cured the ailment in the past; so to be sure, it was generally best to use all of them.

Bee stings were common in a day when nearly all children went barefooted in summer. A baking soda compress was about all that was necessary.

Once or twice all the girls got head lice from a family that lived across the road. Kerosene was the remedy here with a good liberal sousing of the hair with soapy water, and a thorough going through the hair daily with a fine-tooth comb that caught lice and nits. Nits are like rabbits—very prolific, and if not caught in time another crop of lice will emerge. Daily vigilance was the price of liberty. And the fine-tooth comb was an ever-present tool. It was torture to have to be combed and combed and raked and raked every day when a good

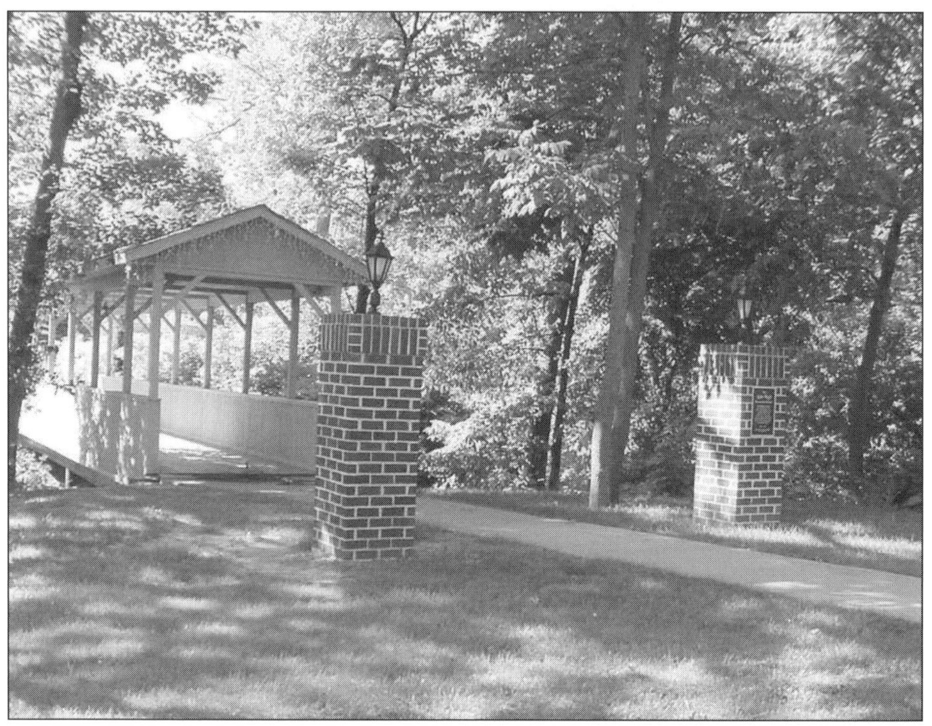

Roeser's Gully can still be seen today. The natural deep drainage ditch is part of the Freeland Memorial Park, separating the park. However, this charming covered bridge provides an easy walkway from one side of the park to the other. Ederer Collection

barn was coaxing to be played in.

Cuts were treated with turpentine. Whether the turpentine was infallible or whether blood was pure—cuts usually healed in short time. Then, as now, bad bruises were treated with cold compresses.

They were not a family of nose bleeders so that remedy could be spared. One winter day Murl started home with Gertie after Sunday school. Kittie was home that day because of illness. In Roeser's Gully near Freeland Murl fell, bumping her nose on the ice. Her nose bled profusely but instead of going home she walked the three-quarters mile to the Lewis house, holding her nose tightly all the way. By the time they reached home her nose was twice as big than it should be and as black and blue as though it had been pounded. The blood had clotted in great blobs like chunks of raw liver.

Mother treated Murl's nose but Murl had a physique that seemed to resist almost everything. Everything—except a pin! At a social at Retta Bishop's house Murl had her back to Kittie. Her back was so plump and tempting that Kittie wondered if she would feel it if she stuck a pin in it. She did! Murl turned on her and gave her a piece of her mind. Kittie should have had a pin stuck in her scrawny little back. She really thought that Murl was so plump that she wouldn't feel the pin. Kittie never wanted to hurt anyone intentionally.

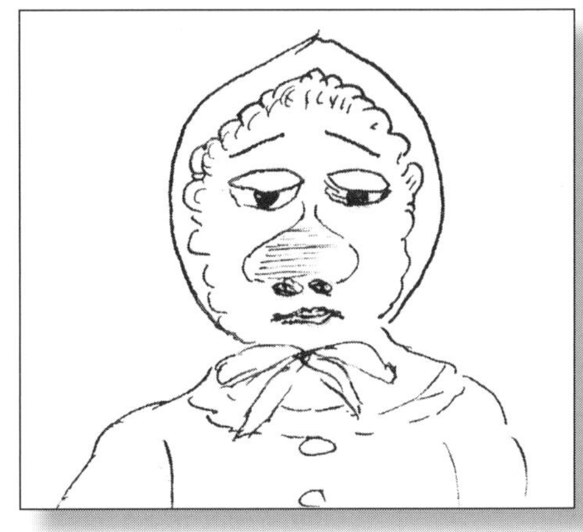

For an upset stomach baking soda and water were the cure all. This was better in action and result than a stomach pump.

Sniffing and sniffing at a camphor bottle usually relieved a headache. Aunt Josie had a great big camphor bottle—something like a whiskey bottle. Smelling of that bottle was a favorite sport of the girls when they were over there. The hired girl must have grown tired of this procedure, and when their smelling was prolonged beyond a reasonable time she said one day, "If you smell camphor too long you're apt to have convulsions." Convulsions! Those things sounded awful, so the cork was twisted in the bottle's neck and it was placed in its usual place before any convulsions could develop.

Flaxseed poultices were used to bring boils, carbuncles and such things to a head. If the poultice itself wouldn't do it—the smell would. It had a very sickening, disagreeable odor—which must have been awful to sleep with.

Then there was the charm or fetish that some children wore to ward off diseases—the "fetty bag." This was worn around the neck in a small bag under the clothing. It was hidden from sight but not from smell. It smelled something like putty mixed with linseed oil. Any germ bold enough to attack a child with a fetty bag was brave indeed! If a child with a fetty bag didn't catch the measles or other contagious diseases it must have been because the child's olfactory nerves didn't allow him to get close enough to get a germ. The girls were thankful they didn't have to wear one. It was bad enough to have to sit within a rod of anyone who wore one.

Uncle Herbert was sick one summer. Mother went down one morning to see how he was getting along. She found him seated on a chair in the kitchen his eyes bulging and his tongue hanging out with its skin hanging in shreds. Instead of his medicine he had taken ammonia by mistake.

Aunt Mary sat with the Doctor Book in her lap reading aloud the symptoms of one who has taken poison. "The skin gets cold and clammy," it said. "Yes," she said, feeling of his face, "You're getting cold and clammy."

Louise was crying when Mother arrived and said, "Well, I guess Pa's goose is cooked this time." They explained what had happened and Mother said, "Well, my land, what are you doing about it? Are you just going to sit there and let him die?"

They gave him the recommended antidote. Then Mother fled for home and dispatched Father off for Dr. Cubbage with the horse on the run. Father brought him back pronto. Doctor said they had given him the right first aid, and after further treatment, he recovered after a few days. Louise's prediction had proven false—he hadn't cooked his goose this time.

One dares not think what might have happened to families in those days when there were no telephones without Dr. Gunn's Home Remedies in his book, *The Family Physician*!

NOTES

Roeser's Gully was next to Roeser's property—his home and store located on Main Street next to the Tittabawassee River. Freeland's Memorial Park is located on the site today and it has been named a Michigan Historic Site. The gully was a very deep ditch, which collected the water and drained into the Tittabawassee River. During winter time the water in the ditch would freeze.

This was the era when people doctored themselves at home. Newspapers advertised the standard home remedies of the day—quinine, sulphur, camphor, turpentine. All of them were very easy to purchase and were usually found in every home's medicine chest. When all else failed, the doctor would be called. The doctor made house calls. Patients didn't go to his home for treatment. Country doctors didn't have offices.

Chapter 21

New Hats and New Horizons

During Sunday school session an announcement was made of a future attraction—A Sunday school excursion to Bay Port. The name "Bay Port" had a magical sound! The excursion train would start from Ludington and stop at the stations along the Pere Marquette Railway—and home again—all in one day! Preposterous! Saginaw had been the extent of trips away from home, and a cutter ride the fastest ride the girls had ever had (except the trip to Grand Ledge and Wacousta on the train when they were too young to remember). And now a train was going to whirl them away to ports unknown! A landlubber planning her first voyage abroad couldn't possibly have been as excited as the Sunday school children. Goose pimples ran up and down their spines just thinking about it.

Father worked hard to get his farm work done so he could take the day off. But the girls knew later in life that he wouldn't have disappointed them even if the work suffered for it.

Somewhere Mother had read or heard of crepe paper hats for little girls. Probably the *Hearth And Home* magazine had advocated this new innovation. The storekeepers gave her five cardboard cracker barrel tops, which became the foundation for the hats. A hole was cut in the center and a puffy crown made to fit over it. Then strips of crepe paper were ruffled and sewed, layer after layer, around the cracker barrel tops.

This meant hours of extra work for Mother but she always enjoyed doing anything that would contribute to children's happiness, whether they were her own or someone else's. After a lot of hard work the hats were finished and really very beautiful—a regular rainbow display with a red one for Carrie Haviland;

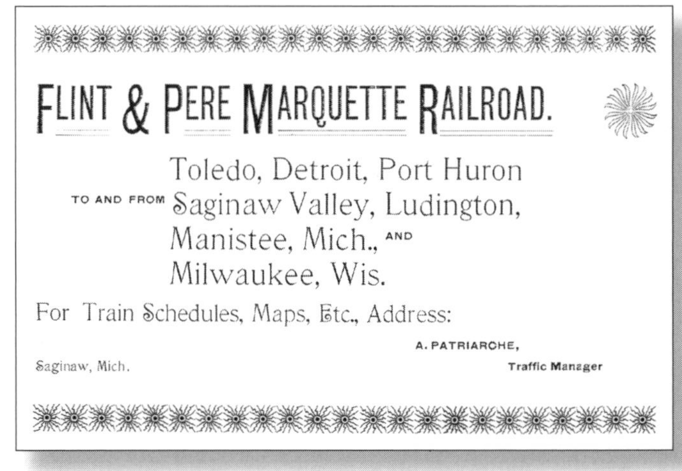
FLINT & PERE MARQUETTE RAILROAD.
TO AND FROM Toledo, Detroit, Port Huron
Saginaw Valley, Ludington,
Manistee, Mich., AND
Milwaukee, Wis.
For Train Schedules, Maps, Etc., Address:
A. PATRIARCHE,
Saginaw, Mich.
Traffic Manager

The F&PM RR provided fast, easy transportation to residents throughout Michigan, to Ohio and Wisconsin. The railroad was the only way to travel any distance since the automobile had not yet been invented. A late 1800s ad.

Eddy Historical Collection

pink for Gertie and Louise; white for Murl and blue for Kittie. They could just visualize the dash they were going to cut in their new finery.

Then the worry! What if it should rain? It would ruin their new millinery and their complexions and hair! Never were skies scanned more often or more anxiously than the day preceding the excursion.

Kittie had that kind of stomach that never could stand too much anticipation. The day before she was alternately crying and vomiting because of a "bilious spell." Her stomach seemed to have an agitator in it like the early washing machine that succeeded the galvanized tub and washboard. Alternate doses of bicarbonate soda and castor oil appeared to get her "unbilious."

Excitement had driven sleep away and several times during the long night the girls had risen to see if the sky was clear or clouds had obliterated the stars. But morning found the girls in high feather. Sunny and bright!

It was a colorful crew that rode to the depot on a morning fairly dripping with sunshine. It would be difficult to tell which shone brighter—the sun or their countenances under the bright, colorful hats.

Father left the horse, old Nell, in Mr. Bishop's barn after depositing his expectant passengers at the depot already bulging at the seams with the motley crowd assembled there. Mothers, fathers, uncles, aunts, brothers, sisters, cousins, friends! The ticket agent was swamped with tickets passing through his iron-barred window.

Many were waiting outside watching up the railroad track. Minutes dragged and excitement was just reaching the boiling point when there, in the

The railroad station shown in the background behind the Old Feed Mill on Depot Street is where the Lewis family and friends would have boarded their train to begin their exciting journey. This elevator was built in 1893 by the Bay City Grain Co. It subsequently became the Dietiker-Howd Elevator. Farmers with their teams and wagons have queued outside the Mill waiting their turn for service. Vasold Collection

distance, was a curl of smoke; a long Too-o-o-o! Too-o-o-o! Toot! Too-o-o-o! as the engine came to a crossing. Then the shining headlight of the locomotive came into view growing larger and larger with every revolution of the wheels. Another loud blast of the whistle and the engine came to a standstill with a hiss-s-s-s-s as the brakes were applied. The engine bell was clanging its merry ding-dong as the crowd surged and pushed toward the train.

The jolly conductor calling, "ALL ABOARD," stood in his blue uniform beside the step that had been placed on the ground to enable passengers to reach the bottom step with ease. The engineer's chubby, good-natured face beamed from the cab as he waved a friendly greeting to excursionists hastening to the train with lunch baskets and boxes.

Lunch boxes, men's hats, and other impedimenta were cached in the racks above the windows. And never was Aladdin's lamp rubbed more lovingly than little fingers rubbed the red plush upholstered seats. And by turning one seat backward a family could sit together, which was conducive to a feeling of security when riding in one of these new-fangled contraptions (at least new to most of the children).

The whistle blew, the bell rang, and they started to move—the thrill of all

The F&PM train would have arrived at this Potter Street Depot in East Saginaw after leaving Freeland. The Railroad's main offices were at this depot. The train then switched cars to the ST&H RR and continued its journey to Bay Port, stopping at several towns. After merging with other railroads, F&PM became the PM RR in 1900. Slasinski Collection

thrills! As the train picked up momentum, the fence posts and telegraph poles whizzed past at a tremendous speed compared to that of old Nell's. Shortly the train passed through Saginaw and then into uncharted territory unfamiliar to the girls.

More people boarded the train at almost every station. It looked as though the Bay Port picnic grounds would be competing with the old woman who lived in the shoe. Coming in sight of Saginaw Bay the girls thought that big expanse of water must be the ocean. They had traveled a long way in a short time, they thought. Then the train ran up into what appeared to be a big woods by the Bay. The conductor called, "ALL CHANGE!" The train screeched to a standstill and there they were at the terminal—Bay Port!

Early breakfasts, high-geared excitement, and the long ride had whetted appetites. After stretching cramped legs, visiting the toilets and washing up a bit picnic lunches vanished and an afternoon of exploration and fun was ahead. No merry-go-rounds—no special attractions! But it was fun just being at the

BAY PORT HOTEL,

On Wild Fowl Bay, Lake Huron,

Situated in a Beautiful Evergreen Grove, at Bay Port, Huron County, Mich., on the line of the Saginaw, Tuscola & Huron Railroad, 46 miles from East Saginaw. This Hotel is New and Strictly First-class. Accommodations for 300 Guests.

A Delightful Resting Place for the Summer Vacation. *THIRD SEASON.*

FINEST YACHTING ON THE GREAT LAKES.

Unexcelled for Fishing, Bathing, Boating, etc., Pure Water, Bracing Air, and Every Facility for Amusement and Recreation.

RATES: $2 a Day and Upwards. Special Terms to Families and for Board by the Week.

For further particulars, address

D. H. WEBSTER, Manager,

Bay Port, Huron County, Mich.

The ST&H RR had a direct line to Bay Port Hotel on Wild Fowl Bay in Lake Huron. The Hotel was a luxurious summer resort patronized by Saginaw's lumbermen during the lumber heyday. The Freeland church group would have spent their day at the beach park, not the Hotel, on Wild Fowl Bay. An 1870s advertisement. Eddy Historical Collection

end of the world!

There were bathing beaches and bathhouses, sailboats and rowboats, and gulls flying here and there screeching in their high-pitched voices. And with Kittie's lively imagination she could see many things that were not there.

Day's end came all too soon and a tired but happy crowd was being transported homeward. It began to grow dark and Kittie was intrigued with the lights at the top of the coach. Many made their way to little rooms at the end of the coach marked: "WOMEN" and "MEN." What a handy contrivance to have on the train! And why was it kept locked at station stops? There was food for thought. And horror of horrors! What if one got locked in there? Kittie thought it safer to stay on this side of that door.

What a wonderful day it had been. Bay Port was now but a treasured memory. But every day after that when the trains blew their whistles they became the symbols of New Horizons. The next excursion was to Port Huron and the most memorable memory of that trip was the beautiful, beautiful blue water of St. Clair River, so much bluer than the Bay or Lake.

The next time the excursion train went to Bay Port Father and Mother didn't go. Mr. Cline, the teacher, said he would take care of the girls. As a special treat for that lunch Kittie wanted bologna sandwiches. Ham, chicken, and pork were so ordinary on the farm but bologna was something special! Kittie and Floyd and their Father were very fond of it.

After lunch Mr. Cline wanted to take the girls for a boat ride. Kittie didn't want to go because she knew from a previous experience what moving along so close to the water did to her sensitive stomach. But he was looking after them so she thought she had to go.

More and more, higher and higher the waves seemed to be coming up in her face. The higher they came the dizzier she became. Just as she thought the waves and her face were going to meet, the boat would give a lurch and they'd ride over the top of the waves. Over and over she experienced this dizzying sensation. Then that churning, pounding feeling in her—well, for politeness' sake we'll call it stomach—but it was lower down. Was it the dizzying effect of the never-ending waves, or could it be the bologna sandwich? Perhaps a combination of the two. She began to wish she had stayed home.

Then on the crowded train Kittie had to sit backward with her back to the engine. The more those telegraph poles and trees receded in the background (foreground, really, to her) the faster her head and stomach whirled. Mr. Cline saw her face taking on a sickly green hue—and white about the gills. And he succeeded in opening the window just in time for the bologna sandwich and other treats to be heaved overboard—to her relief, if not to those about her!

For a long, long time rowboats, bologna, and riding backwards brought very unpleasant associations and memories.

NOTES

The Saginaw, Tuscola & Huron Railroad was organized in 1881 with Jesse Hoyt being the largest stockholder. Rail tracks were built from East Saginaw to various cities as follows: to Sebewaing in 1882, to Bay Port and Stone Quarry in 1883, to Wild Fowl Bay in 1884, to Bad Axe in 1886. This new railroad also ran past several rural villages—Reese, Fairgrove, Akron, and Unionville. Crushed stone from Stone Quarry was brought by rail to Saginaw and Bay Counties for the macadam road building in the early 1900s. The railroad opened up new horizons for these rural communities, and people often boarded the train to come to Saginaw for parades, circuses, or other events.

The Flint & Pere Marquette Railroad's main offices were at Washington & Potter Streets in East Saginaw. This railroad leased the ST&H tracks until purchasing them for one million dollars on January 4, 1900. The Flint & Pere Marquette Railroad developed a summer resort at Bay Port. Located on the eastern side of Saginaw Bay, Wild Fowl Bay had a natural harbor ideal for sailing, hunting, fishing, and bathing. The train apparently stopped at several small rural communities along the route and several people boarded for an all-day excursion. Wild Fowl Bay is probably where the Freeland church group also spent their day. The railroad also built the Bay Port Hotel, a very luxurious summer resort, on the high south shore in 1886. Many wealthy lumber barons' families from Saginaw would spend several weeks during the summer at this hotel-resort.

The Flint & Pere Marquette also had a direct line to Port Huron, several Canadian cities, Buffalo and the East. The Flint & Pere Marquette Railroad Company had been organized in 1857 to build a road from Flint to Pere Marquette (Ludington). After Jesse Hoyt rescued the railroad from receivership in 1879, it became one of Michigan's major roads. It also was an important logging train, bringing timber to Saginaw River sawmills. Between 1867 and 1872 road had been laid from East Saginaw to Midland to Averill to Clare and Bay City. This is the railroad that passed through Freeland, bypassing Loretto, in 1867. After consolidating with other railroads, it became the Pere Marquette Railroad on January 7, 1900. The Chesapeake & Ohio bought the Pere Marquette in 1947. Passenger service was discontinued in 1950.

Wacousta is an unincorporated community in Watertown Township in Clinton County. Eagle Michigan is the nearest town. Wacousta has a population of 4,162 today. A Post Office had been established in Wacousta in 1839.

Before the days of electricity, this is the type of sewing machine Katie Lewis would have used. It is operated by a foot pedal and hand wheel, as seen in this Morley Brothers advertisement. Morley Companies Collection

Chapter 22

Mother's Dilemma

Mother stood at the dining room table with puckered brow, a look of weariness and anxiety on her face. Narrow gores and gores of pretty cloth lay spread out on the table with pieces of tissue pattern laid this way and that way to no avail. It just couldn't be done! Try as hard as she would she couldn't see how that pattern was going to transform Aunt Ellen's old dress into a new one for Kittie. In desperation and exasperation she finally said, "Maybe if your Aunt Ellen knew your middle name is Ellen, she'd buy you a new dress!"

Something clicked in Kittie's brain. This wise bit of inspiration was stored away for future use—to take root at the proper time. By pinning a piece of cloth on this gore and another one on that gore Mother at last managed to cut out a dress.

Mother was an A#1 dressmaker (necessity is the mother of invention) and with a whole piece of new material could really go to town. Aunt Ellen had married a well-to-do farmer and lumberman, so her dresses and coats were always made of very good material. Eventually they found their way to our house and Mother was very thankful to have such nice material to eke out the girls' wardrobes.

But a great deal of work was involved. Coats and dresses must be ripped, steamed, pressed, laid out to best advantage, and must find a pattern that would best adapt itself to the material on hand. Often it was no trick at all. But a skirt with many narrow gores required all her ingenuity—plus!

Mother had a good Domestic sewing machine and she could make that thing fairly brindle. She could wind a bobbin quicker than you can say Jack

Robinson. It was a treadle machine; and in starting it she gave the little upper wheel at the right a push—at the same time treading the treadle with her foot and—clickety-click—she had that thing going lickety-split in split seconds.

Gertie could use the old Domestic fairly well, but whenever Kittie tried to use it she invariably broke the thread because she couldn't keep the wheel and the treadle going at the same time. It was like rubbing your head and stomach at the same time. When sewing is involved, her motor coordination has always been disgraceful.

The girls were seldom in a Ladies' or Children's Apparel Establishment until they began teaching. In fact, children's clothes were seldom ready made in those days. And yet they were well dressed. Mother could make pin tucks, ruffling, shirring, smocking, hemstitching, or any other stitch that was then in existence. She was a cracker jack!

Aunt Mary did all her sewing on our old Domestic. Day after day she'd be there sewing. One day Mother had planned a good day's sewing and had the machine and materials ready. Just as things were well under way, in walked Aunt Mary with her sewing. "Well," she said, "I wanted to sew today." For once Mother asserted her rights and replied, "Well, I'm using the machine today myself." And she stuck to her guns. Aunt Mary went away ruffling her feathers—mad as an old wet hen. Many years later when Aunt Mary bought her new White Sewing Machine, she hugged it to herself and never once said, "I've used yours for so many years, now you come down and use mine." On, no! Not Aunt Mary! Her motto was, "Get all you can for as little as you can."

All her life Mother got so much pleasure in sharing with and doing for others. Her wealth was in kind deeds rather than in material possessions.

NOTES

Women's and children's clothing and baby diapers were not bought ready made during the 1800s. Everything was sewn by hand, and the treadle sewing machine was the most helpful invention for dressmakers. Every community had its dressmakers and milliners. A city as large as Saginaw had several. Many women in the 1800s made their livelihood by sewing clothing and making hats for others. The ordinary women and farmers' wives

This photo of Katie Lewis was taken in her later years, about 1943.

usually sewed their own family's clothing. Dry goods stores sold the cloth from bolts of fabric, and women would purchase material to sew their own clothing.Freeland Village had one or two dressmakers and millinery shops on Washington Street. They were probably busy sewing clothing and hats for the well-to-do women such as Aunt Ellen Hackett or the shopkeepers' wives. Katie Allen was a farmer's wife with limited income, and she had to make do with second-hand clothing from others, especially from her sister, Ellen Hackett.

Chapter 23

The Annual Visit

The time had come for the two-day visit to Aunt Ellen's. Mother took the girls the two and one-half miles with old Nell and stayed until afternoon. Life at Aunt Ellen's was rather complex compared to theirs.

Uncle John owned nearly a section of land—some 300 acres. Father had 20 acres and worked 51 acres for Grandpa Lewis. Uncle John employed about fifteen men the year round. In summer they worked on the farm, and in winter most of them worked in his lumber camp near Averill.

The girls always visited in summer so they saw many activities going on. There were many buildings on the farm: horse barns, cow barns, granary, corn crib, tool shed, hen houses and chicken coops, pig pens, smoke house, ice house, men's house, and perhaps others.

Gertie and Kittie knew old Ringer better than the other men. He was the "chore boy" as he was called. They were fascinated with his swill-barrel cart, and followed him faithfully as he wheeled it from place to place talking to himself as he walked. At home all the swill (pigs' feed) was carried by hand in pails. But Ringer would fill up his barrels wheeling the cart to the pig sty and pouring the swill into the troughs where, pig fashion, the greedy, squealing hogs noisily gobbled it up—slopping it on one another's ears and snouts in the process.

Ringer was a good steady worker when sober but he would imbibe, and then he became quite garrulous and not too dependable. Then one of the other men had to take over. The girls had frequently seen him lying in Roeser's or Uncle Guy's Gully in a stupor after one of his regular trips to the saloon. They would pick up chunks of clay and throw them, hitting him on the shoes or legs.

He'd rouse to a sitting position and shout, and the girls would run for their lives. But they had their fear for nothing—he couldn't even walk, to say nothing of running, until the torpor of his brain cleared up.

At Aunt Ellen's the men were always fed first. A long table extended nearly the length of the kitchen. In winter the cooking was done in the same room on a large wood range, as there were fewer men to cook for. In the summer this was done in the summer kitchen, which was a combination kitchen and woodshed adjoining the kitchen, and here were stoves, tables, and a general work area. The kitchen end was on a long platform built a few feet higher than the woodshed.

Aunts Ellen and Pollie and the hired girl (they only had one kind of maids in those days—old ones!) spent practically all their time over a hot fire on the hottest days, preparing and cooking meat and vegetables; kneading and baking loaf after loaf of good bread; baking pies, white cookies, molasses cookies; and frying fried cakes and doughnuts in a huge kettle of sizzling hot lard.

The men from the barns and fields splashed and washed in washbasins in the men's house or out doors, drying their bewhiskered faces on a large roller towel. As they filed into the kitchen one by one Aunt Ellen or someone stood at the door and shook a fly apparatus (a lot of ribbon-like papers fastened to a stick) to shoo the flies, which were always plentiful on farms. The house was some distance from the barns—nevertheless swarms and swarms of flies were always on hand to sample a few morsels of the good food. Uncle John believed in keeping his men well fed. It took hours to prepare the food that those hungry men gobbled down in short order. The table was cleared and then the women and children could eat.

Off of a hallway between kitchen and dining room was a pantry as large as a modern kitchen, with cupboards and work counters on three sides. Usually before dinner or supper was ready Kittie would walk back and forth past that door, looking in at Aunt Pollie sugaring doughnuts. After a few trips she'd venture in a small soft voice, "I know what's in that big can. You keep white cookies in there. And you keep molasses cookies in that other can. That can over there has fried cakes in it." All of this must have been big news to Aunt Pollie.

"Would you like a cookie?" good Aunt Pollie would say. "And a fried cake?" "I don't care," Kittie would reply—but of course she did care. She was starved. At home the girls could stay their hunger between meals with a slice of home made bread and butter covered with brown sugar—a delicious treat they liked. Then the cookies and fried cakes were handed out for both girls. Kittie never could figure out the mystery—how could Aunt Pollie know she was hungry? One time when she was very young Aunt Ellen was flaking codfish and she gave her a piece. Kittie took it out in the yard and buried it (from the smell and taste she thought it was dead) and then when she got a chance she whispered to her Mother, telling her it tasted like cat dung. How did she know that when she never tasted that! She was too young to remember that but it tickled Mother.

Dishes, dishes, dishes! Kettles, pots, pans! All the water heated on the cook stove and no new, new Ivory Liquid to keep hands as soft as your face! But nothing for the girls to do but explore. The smokehouse, a red brick building with a roof similar to Purchase's privy, and a small window up high was a great attraction. "What a nice playhouse if we could go in," they said. But the door was locked and the window way out of reach. Gertie tried in vain to boost Kittie up so she could see inside. Probably a lot of hams and bacon in the curing process.

Uncle John had a lawnmower for his huge lawn—a thing unknown in the girls' quarter of the globe. A scythe came the closest to a lawnmower by the Allen and Lewis relatives who hadn't married into the lumbering industry. A high, wide boardwalk led from the front porch to the road several rods away. Kittie pushed that lawnmower up and down the walk pretending it was a baby buggy. The height of her ambition was to own a doll buggy—but one that never was realized. That lawn mower came the closest to it of anything she had seen.

Tiring of that, a walk down the east road toward the O'Donnell house—the only house in that mile. But greatest of all attractions was the ferry at the foot of the gully south of Aunt Ellen's house. This was a windlass affair operated by the Kapitan family who lived across the river and who ferried passengers, teams and vehicles across the Tittabawassee River. More than anything the girls wanted a ride on that ferry. They were fairly green with envy when they saw other people riding across. It couldn't have held more than two

Martin Kapitan operated this toll ferry where the present-day Tittabawassee Bridge crosses the river. Seen here in the 1880s, he would pull on the cable attached to each side of the riverbank to bring the barge and passengers to the opposite side. The ferry service was discontinued when the bridge was built in 1909. Vasold Collection

or three vehicles at the most. In later years Aunt Ellen wished she had known they wanted a ride—she would have taken them across gladly. That was an age when children were seen and not heard—at least when they were away from home. So that was one thrill they never experienced. The landing was between two high, steep banks, which the girls named Green Mountains and White Mountains. Evidently Gertie had gleaned a little from *Harper's Old Geography!* At the landing on this side, roads went to the right and left up the slopes to the main road. The girls would walk down the first road to the landing and stand looking across the river where the ferry was waiting. One of the Kapitan's would come out of the shanty on the bank and start toward the ferry. Then their feet would quicken their pace, as they'd take the other road up to the main road and past the Mountains again. Ferry service was discontinued after the bridge was built.

Close to the house was the milk house, quite a building in itself. The girls can still remember the smell to this day. Not unpleasant like warm milk which is so cowy. This house had a cooling system where milk was kept in big zinc-lined bins. The milk and cream were separated in here. The skimmed milk was fed to calves, pigs and chickens, and made into Dutch cheese for the table; the cream, into butter.

Mother had a stone churn with a churn dasher (chay-daddle) for butter making. But Aunt Ellen had a barrel churn with a crank on one side that turned the churn end over end with every whirl of the crank. On the cover of the churn was a little round window where little blobs of butter gathered to announce that the butter had come. If one forgot to anchor the churn with a hook before removing the cover, the greasy contents were spilled on the floor. (This happened to a friend of the family who was having several guests for supper—all that mess to clean up besides getting ready for company.)

Later on the Lewis family had a barrel churn, which was easier than pushing a dasher up and down for endless minutes, but it still was work to keep it turning over and over with its heavy load (but excellent for burning up calories). It's so much easier today to walk into a supermarket, slide a glass door and select a pound of butter, which is kept refrigerated. But the rich reward is missing—a drink of that delicious buttermilk. It had little globules of butter that wouldn't stick to the ladle floating in it. Oh, for a drink of good, cold homemade buttermilk. People weren't concerned about hardening of the arteries or the circulatory troubles of the present day. And no one seemed to be calorie conscious. Everything was cooked (fried) in or with butter or lard and no one had to worry about it. Being "on a diet" was unheard of. In spite of the fact that "Crisco is the shortening so fresh, so white, so digestible—the shortening that gives you confidence," there were cooks with plenty of confidence gained from using pure homemade lard years before Crisco was ever thought of or heard of. Getting back to the milk house—a step or two led down into a pit or lower floor presumably for the drainage pipes from the cooling system. The girls didn't understand the intricacies of that part. Like gravity, it was there but not understood.

Weary with all the walking they had done, the girls went to bed early in a bedroom up the back stairway. Aunt Pollie slept in a room near them. Aunt Pollie had long brown hair, so long she could sit on it, and they loved to watch her brush and comb it, braiding it and twisting it into a big pug or bun on the back. She was very pretty with clear white skin, kind, blue eyes, and a kindly smile. Kittie decided she was going to be tall and look like her when she grew up only she wanted to have longer teeth! As more people came into her young life she periodically changed her ideas of how she was going to look. Maybe that is why she was so plain looking when she grew up—perhaps she was just a conglomeration of the many people she had admired without having the nice identity of any of them.

Morning came and with it the same old routine. Breakfast over and dishes washed Aunt Ellen and the hired girl began preparing vegetables and things for the noon meal. Aunt Pollie went to the men's house northeast of the house with the girls tagging at her heels. This was a good-sized house with one room upstairs and one downstairs. The downstairs was a living room, lounging room, and washroom; and upstairs beds and beds in rows with the bedding in an upheaval which told that the men slept there. Aunt Pollie had all these beds to make every day. Not a very pleasant task for one who was spinster by name and spinster by nature. Mother told Kittie years later that some of these men weren't very nice men. And all that bedding to keep clean in a hand propelled washing machine—without the three-ring agitator of the automatic Frigidaire today!

Eggs to gather in row after row of hens' nests. Dozens and dozens of eggs every day, and this, too, was Aunt Pollie's job. Some hens with the strong motherly instinct were determined to "set", and when she'd reach under them to get the eggs or to pull the hens off the nest they'd ruffle their feathers around their necks, spread their stiff wings in defiance and making a raspy cr-r-r-r-sound would peck her hands in retaliation. Not a very enviable job!

In the dining room that they used as a living room (except on rare occasions when the parlor was opened) was a mantel on which was a lovely clear glass sailboat in a bottle. Kittie admired this boat every time she went there trying to solve the mystery—how did the boat ever get into that bottle? It was a full rigged sailboat and she couldn't see how those thin, threadlike masts could have been pushed through the bottle's neck without being broken. But she wouldn't

have thought of asking why. Neither would she hint that she'd love to hold it in her hands. "Theirs not to reason why—theirs but to do or die" was the psychology of the time. It is very evident why children of today's generation learn more than those 50 or 60 years ago. Then it was: "Touch not, taste not, handle not." But today it seems to be: "Don't repress the child—never say 'Don't' to a child. Give him opportunity for self expression."

When Uncle John would appear at the house, he'd say, "Hello, little boys." Now if there's anything a little girl hates it's being called a boy. The girls wouldn't have cared if he had said "tomboys"—they knew they were that—but just plain "boys" were insulting! They never had any real affection for him or he for them. Mother had married the man of her choice instead of the one Uncle John had selected for her, and that was almost unforgivable!

Uncle John was noted for his fine horses, among the best in the country. When they drove a span hitched to their fine carriage they really went places in elegant style. Since mechanized machinery hadn't yet come into their own, it was necessary to keep many workhorses on a farm that size. All farm work was done in a slow, laborious manner. Plowing, dragging, planting, cultivating, harvesting, hauling—all were done with horses. That was why it was necessary to keep so many men on his farm. It was fun watching farm operations on such a large scale—but it would be fun to get home again where they could be their natural free selves once more.

Aunt Ellen let them go up the long, stately front stairway into the attic. There they found some old hats and clothes to dress up in. Seeing the dresses and other garments there, Kittie said, "Ma said maybe if you knew my middle name is Ellen you might get up a new dress." She did! (Fools and children walk where angels fear to tread.)

After two days and nights it was a relief to see Mother and old Nell heaving in sight. Another year would pass before they'd be visiting these exciting haunts again!

Home again, Kittie had a new interest that had been born while watching Aunt Pollie clean her birdcage. She had a canary with a beautiful voice. It would sing by the hour. She told Kittie if she could catch a bird she would give her a cage. And that little girl was determined to own that birdcage. Somewhere she had heard that if you could put salt on a bird's tail you could catch it. If that was all, she was going to have a bird and a birdcage. She dashed into the house, took a fistful of salt from her mother's salt dish and went out stalking birds. Ah! There was a robin on the ground just a few feet away! Tiptoeing cautiously she threw the salt but it landed—not on the tail but on the spot where the robin had been.

Into the house and out again Kittie went with another fistful of salt. She chased and threw, chased and threw, but the birds were all alike—they wouldn't hold their tails still long enough. Hot, tired, and disheveled, she gave up until another day. This went on for several days with salt disappearing like water down a drain. At last she relinquished all hope of a bird or a birdcage. Birds were too quick with their tails. Probably salt wouldn't stay on if you could throw it on its tail. That rule wouldn't hold water. Someone must have lied to her! She was learning more and more through her many experiments.

NOTES

John Hackett was considered a wealthy, prosperous farmer lumberman in the 1890s. He owned two parcels of land on either side of the Midland Road and extending to the Tittabawassee River. Because everything—both farm and household—was all done manually, he hired several men who lived on his farm. The men worked in his lumber camp in Averill during the winter months. Averill was located north of Midland on the Tittabawassee River. Averill was a large banking ground. Logs were brought from many rivers upstream and piled here until springtime. Timber was also harvested here, and then it would be transported on the river in the spring. His Freeland property was next to the present-day Tittabawassee Road, and it was some distance from the Lewis home near Pierce Road.

Lumber camps such as this one were built in Averill and throughout central Michigan. The lumber camp owner hired shanty boys to cut down the large pine trees from November through March. Then the logs would be floated down the rivers to the Tittabawassee and eventually to the Saginaw River sawmills. John Hackett also operated a lumber camp in Averill during the winter months, using the same work crew that worked on his farm during the summer months. Slasinski Collection

Freeland was located on both sides of the Tittabawassee River. Because there were no bridges, residents had to cross the river by canoes or ferries. Martin Kapitan and his brothers operated a ferry that crossed the river where the Tittabawassee Bridge was later built. It was located about three and one-half miles down the river from the Freeland Village. This is the ferry mentioned in this chapter. This ferry operated until 1909 when a bridge was built in its place. Orrie Crampton operated another ferry crossing the river by Pierce Road about one mile south of Freeland for a short time.

Chapter 24

From Old to New Dresses

If... *Little drops of water, little grains of sand,*
Make the mighty ocean, and the pleasant land...then
Little hints given when Aunt Ellen was near
Brought brand new dresses
To three little girls so dear.

Kittie's timely remark quoting her mother on old dresses versus new ones—brought its reward. Aunt Ellen came up one day a veritable fairy godmother whose magic wand in the shape of a purse produced yards of cashmere material and silk and lace trimming for three new dresses: A green one with changeable silk for Gertie; one for Louise; and a plum color with plum and gold changeable silk and cream-colored lace for Kittie.

It would be difficult to tell who was the happiest—the giver, the girls, or Mother. The joy of laying a pattern on a piece of whole new cloth, and the pleasure of sewing the cloth, silk and lace of such rich texture were beyond description. When the dresses were finished, Mother said the girls must have their pictures taken. That meant a trip to Saginaw on the train.

Gertie was the first to go. Father only took Gertie this time. On the train he left Gertie alone while he went into the smoker. She always had a fear of trains. If the family was going to go anywhere in the buggy, she would always throw up her hands, take a quick breath and say, "Oh, will we have to cross a railroad?" If they did, it took the pleasure out of a trip for her. It is thought that her fear dated back to the day one of Floyd's schoolmates, Bert Vanluven, was killed while trying to catch a ride on a freight train on the way home from school.

Gertie worried for fear Father wouldn't be back when they reached Saginaw. What would she do? He was on hand before the train stopped, but she had a very serious expression on her young face in that picture. Adults don't always realize the fears that children have.

Another day Father took Kittie. They walked to the depot about one and one-half miles, and Uncle Guy laughed to see her strutting by in her new finery, a jump ahead of her father as they went by.

Mother had told her to be sure to close her mouth in the picture, and also how she wanted the photographer to arrange her hair. Mother had braided her hair tightly the night before and then unbraided the lower half of her braid, giving it a pretty wavy appearance.

The photographer seated her in a chair. Then Kittie said, "Mamma wants you to put my wavy hair over my shoulder." He did, and then he asked her to smile. But Kittie remembered Mother's advice and closed her lips tightly. Her picture was satisfactory, but her expression as much as said, "You needn't try to flirt with me for I don't know you."

Before the picture-taking spree was over, the photographer had shot pictures of Father, Mother, Uncle Herbert, Aunt Mary, Louise, Uncle Guy, and Aunt Josie. So Kittie's timely hint not only brought new dresses, but photographs of all and for all the relatives. And it must have "swelled" the coffers of the photographer. So she got a new dress if she didn't get a birdcage!

This is Kittie's photo that was taken that day in Saginaw. Her wavy hair had been draped over her left shoulder and tied with a large ribbon. She may have closed her lips tightly, but she certainly is a pretty child.

Freeland always had a band to play at its community celebrations. The Munger Band was a five-piece band. This 1907 Freeland Band also played in many community events. Standing in back row from left to right: (?), leader Frank Winslow, Ray Winslow, Mr. Acker, Albert Vasold, Ross Winslow. 2nd Row: Russell VanBuren, Howard Shaffer, Mr. Acker, Stub Beech, Joe Wickham, (?) (?). Sitting: (?), George King,(?) Vasold Collection

Chapter 25

Fourth of July Celebrations

Fourth of July—Independence Day! A day to anticipate for weeks! Visions went racing through young minds in kaleidoscopic fashion: Picnic dinner, homemade ice cream and lemonade; a bowery; the Munger Band; firecrackers, torpedoes; Roman candles!

Busy days of preparation! As Father caught the chickens and took them to the chopping block, the girls raced into the front bedroom, holding fingers in their ears to shut out the last squawks. But they got out in the yard in time to see the bloody-necked fowls flopping around crazily with their heads off until their stored-up energy was freed.

Mother had the pails of hot water ready in which the chickens had their first full bath. Their feathers, which smelled to high heaven, were soon plucked and there they dangled in their clean, shiny nakedness.

As Mother dressed the fowls (to the girls it seemed more like undressing them) they stood at her elbow watching while she cut open the birds and took out their vital organs and the "innards." Today they are known by a more refined name—intestines. But then they were commonly designated "guts" or "innards." If, however, one broke it smelled the same regardless of which name it was called. They loved to watch her open the gizzard with its opalescent or iridescent colors.

The stock was put in a cool place to thicken. All the meat was taken off the bones and cut into small pieces. Then the meat and the thick, jellied stock were seasoned and packed into an oblong pan and a heavy weight placed upon it. When cooled under the weight, it was pressed chicken and could be sliced like present-day meat loaf. And it was good. Can the health authorities tell

This partial 1896 map indicates that the trip from the Jacob Lewis farm north up Midland Road, west over the Freeland Bridge, down Freeland Road, and to Sam P. Acker's property was indeed a very long trip for a horse and wagon ride, as noted with the heavy black line. Acker's Pine Grove was a quarter mile off the main road to the woods. Vasold Collection

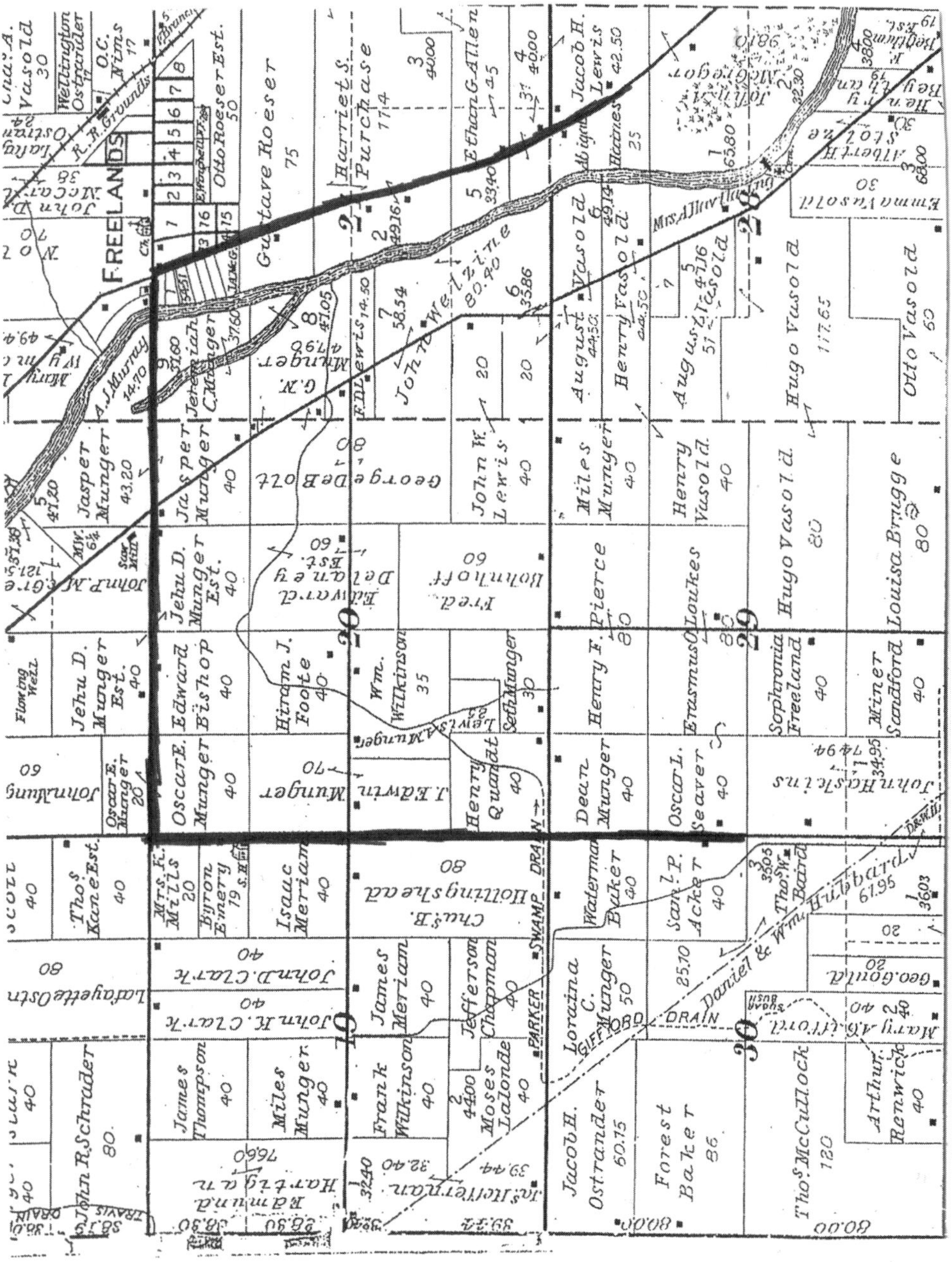

us why chicken prepared the day before with no refrigeration and packed in a basket for a few hours on a hot July day didn't cause ptomaine poisoning sixty years ago, when today most of the crowd would end up in the hospitals? Ignorance was bliss!

Then there were pans of potato salad, deviled eggs, green onions, radishes, pickles, beet pickles, cheese, Dutch (cottage) cheese, homemade bread and butter, or Parker House rolls, baked beans, tarts, fried cakes, cream cake, black raspberry pie, and watermelon—and iced tea for the adults. No waxed paper! No aluminum foil! No saran wrap! But that dinner was as fresh as a daisy in spite of the slogan: "Only aluminum foil keeps the air out and keeps freshness in." Don't get the idea that one family furnished all this food. Several families had their picnic together.

Days and hours dragged but at last the night before arrived. A cloudy sunset and lowering skies! Anxiety spread over the girls' faces and dampened their spirits.

Saturday night or not—baths were the order and clean clothes laid out. Waking early in the morning—the sound of raindrops running down the rain board! Dispositions matched gray skies. But Mother said cheerfully, "Rain before seven, 'twill stop before eleven." Then spirits soared again because "what Ma says is so." And whether it was a woman's intuition, her sixth sense, or her prophetic power it did as she said. Raindrops slackened their pace and output, and a tiny patch of blue appeared in the north sky. Mother cheerfully predicted: "It's going to stop raining. There's enough blue sky in the north to make a Dutchman a pair of breeches (britches)." "Ma is smart and nice—she knows everything," they said. Soon the sky showed enough blue for many pairs of Dutchmen's breeches. The sun shone bright, drying up the raindrops, and Gertie and Kittie were as elated as circus balloons. The picnic was going to come to fruition!

Faces shone with soap and water as well as with joy. Dressed in starched white dresses with hair ribbons and ribbon sashes, would the hour for departure never come! Father drove up in the wagon into which extra seats had been put to hold Aunt Mary, Uncle Herbert, Louise, Murl, and the Lewis family. It seemed an endless ride up to Freeland and across the river to Acker's Pine Grove reached by a quarter mile lane from the main road to the woods. What a thrill when the horses turned into the lane and Old Glory hung there, her red, white and blue waving in all her glory. The bass and snare drums of the Munger Band could be heard in the grove pounding out their patriotism, and even the horses' feet seemed tuned to their rhythmic beat.

Popcorn, ice cream and lemonade stands had been erected and looked as bright in their red, white and blue bunting as a sailor on leave. A mad scramble for the home built tables, which were conspicuous by their scarcity. On such occasions it was not unusual to spread the cloth on the ground—eating Hindu fashion with legs crossed. But the entire Lewis clan opened their many picnic baskets and feasted on the sumptuous food! Other wagons pulled up, and large families brought out their heavy picnic baskets while both young and old feasted on their large spreads.

Dinner over, the oldsters packed away the remnants to be eaten later, and the youngsters were attracted to the popcorn stand where barkers were nearly splitting their throats, calling in their raucous voices, *"POPCORN! RIGHT THIS WAY FOR YOUR FRESH BUTTERED POPCORN!"*

By one or two o'clock patriotic speeches were in order. Speeches then as now were made by political candidates who in stentorian voices were using this patriotic occasion to swell the number of votes at the fall election by shouting at the top of their lungs—"What I believe." The grove beckoned to the young fry who gladly left political speeches to join hands for a walk through the woods. They were just about to step over a long, thick stick when the "stick" moved and a blacksnake raised its head and stuck out its' wicked tongue, wiggling it faster than a tongue hung at both ends. Some of the terrified girls ran for Father, and he and Uncle Will killed the mammoth serpent. Uncle Will held it up by the tail, and it was about six feet long. The girls began to think perhaps orators were safer than six-foot long blacksnakes.

Dance music lured young feet to the bowery where a square dance was getting under way. The caller was calling in an amplified voice, "First two couples lead up to the right," and young ladies in long white, ruffled dresses floated hand in hand with bewhiskered young snappers to the couples on their right. "Do-si-do and all swing around; allemande left," and etc. until every couple had had its turn and all participants wore rapt expressions on their happy faces. Kittie was always very full of rhythm, and as she stood watching the

couples doing the "allemande left" she vowed that when she grew up she would wear a long ruffled dress and dance on a bowery. Her dream never materialized. Boweries were considered common and cheap by that time. When the call was given, "Swing your partner," the young men almost lifted the young ladies off the floor and spun them round and round in a mad whirl that made their balloon dresses balloon out, "exposing their limbs"—how shocking!

By this time politicians were through kissing babies and saying polite nothings. And if their constituents could believe that the politicians believed what they professed to believe—then they could rest assured that the old "Ship of State" would be steered clear of the shoals and would land safely in the harbor in spite of buffetings and unseen dangers. Everyone must have slept more peacefully that night knowing that such stalwart patriotic men were at the helm.

Cows, pigs, and chickens were waiting at home for their Fourth of July dinner. So home for chores and a lunch on the remains of the picnic dinner which had stood in the heat all the afternoon, unaware that staphylococcus germs might be lurking there. People's systems seemed well fortified against the germs and viruses that have come with denser population and more refined foods. The old wheat bin in the granary generously supplied what goes over the druggist's counter today in its enclosed capsule at $7 or $8 per hundred.

Evening coming on, Uncle Herbert, Aunt Mary, and Louise came up to see and hear the small display of firecrackers which had been bought at 5 or

10 cents a bunch. The trick was to light a fuse and throw the cracker before it could explode in one's hands. If it didn't go off instantly, the girls would run to pick it up. But their father cautioned them that sometimes there seemed to be a delayed action and it might discharge when least expected. Floyd showed how putting the lighted cracker under a tin can could produce a small cannon effect. Characteristic of all children the girls liked the bigger noise, and they laughed to see the can tossed into the air by the discharge of the hidden firecracker. Usually when they came to the last bunch their father would leave the bunch together, lighting only one fuse which in turn lighted another until a chain reaction set all the crackers sputtering—and the girls could imagine they were sparklers seen at big fireworks displays elsewhere.

Excitement over—it was time to pile into the wagon again to go to Freeland to see the spectacular fireworks display.

Big giant cannon firecrackers were tossed by teenage boys in the streets scaring little girls who had heard of a girl in Saginaw who had been decapitated by one. No child wanted to donate her head to the cause of liberty, freedom, and independence.

Soon the real fireworks began. A hiss was heard, then a gold snake like trail blazed through the air. And when it burst high in the night sky the crescendo, prolonged oh-h-h-h's and ah-h-h-h's of all ages were evidence of fulfilled anticipation. Then came the sparklers which, fastened to a wheel, gave a crackling sound as the wheel revolved and the fiery sparks rained to the ground like a miniature golden waterfall.

Next those fireworks that were catapulted high into the air at a speed faster then sound. The expectant crowd, with backs of heads resting on their shoulders, waited for the burst which released a shower of colored meteor-like spheres that parachuted to earth—many floating long distances away. More oh-h-h-h's and ah-h-h-h's! A few more set pieces and all was over—all except the delightful smell of gunpowder which tainted and colored the air. Independence Day had brought satisfaction and pleasure to all in a day when outside attractions were almost as scarce as hens' teeth.

Events of the day went racing through Kittie's mind, chasing sleep from her tired body. But when she finally fell asleep she dreamed she was whooshed into space on the snakelike head of a Roman candle, hissing as it burst in the

Whenever there was a large celebration downtown such as the Fourth of July fireworks, the large overflow crowd used all available space to tie their horses, buggies, and wagons. Both the Adventist and Congregational Churches' horse sheds were used. The horse sheds at the Methodist Episcopal Church on Washington & Second Streets were also used.
Freeland United Methodist Church Collection

air with a glorious exhibition of blacksnakes, and landing on the bowery where she was being whirled around and around by a politician who was calling in a hoarse voice, "Right this way for ice cold lemonade!"

Another long remembered Fourth of July was the one that combined a homecoming with a street celebration in Freeland. At that time there were no automobiles and all the horse and buggy traffic was local. Farmers tied their horses to hitching posts, which stood in front of business places. Then for an overflow crowd the Methodist, Adventist, and Congregational Church sheds could shelter many horses that were there for the day.

A sort of viewing stand was erected in the main street where laugh-provoking contests took place. Boys entered the pie-eating contest in which they ate pies from plates without using their hands. Naturally they got more pie on their faces than in their stomachs. Another contest was one in which they ate wind biscuits or crackers until a gong rang as a signal for them to whistle. People were convulsed in laughter as the boys tried in vain to whistle, their lips and throats as dry as in the days of prohibition.

A bandstand was also in the street, and couples were in full swing on the ever-popular bowery.

Greatest of all attractions for Louise and Kittie was the merry-go-round on the vacant lot north of Frank Lewis' store. Their heartbeats quickened and then missed several beats as they listened to the enchantment of the mechanical music in the center of the merry-go-round. Round and round, faster and faster they rode with sparkling eyes and happy faces, trying the various horses as they slid up and down the poles. And such a let down when at last the music and merry-go-round went slower and slower and they had spent their last nickels. They stood looking at their beloved merry-go-round with worshipful eyes as new riders mounted their wooden steeds and whirled away to the same old tune. It stopped and started, stopped and started—and all the time their eyes were hanging out of their cheeks.

A nice looking boy stepped up to Kittie, and telling her he lived at LaPorte invited her to have a ride with him. Momentarily she was undecided, but her mother's teaching had taken root and she refused because she had been told never to talk or ride with a stranger. How was she to know that Mother meant men driving along country roads? Here was a perfectly good merry-go-round, a girl aching for a ride, and a nice appearing, good-looking boy—but he was a stranger and strangers were taboo. When she found her mother she told of her refusal, and Mother said, "Why, it would have been all right for you to ride with him when he asked you." Alas! A good ride gone down the drain!

Kittie was drawn to that merry-go-round as steel to a magnet and stood waiting for a second Prince Charming to come along and ask her. The stars in her eyes must have flagged him for there in front of the girls stood a tall, thin man with light hair and mustache offering them a ride.

Without waiting to analyze what Mother had said, their sprightly steps soon had them on the horses with Old Prince Charming standing between them, a hand on each horse and a big, silly grin on his little, silly face. As the merry-go-round picked up momentum, the girls came in sight of Mother and Uncle Guy who seemed to know where to find them.

As the happy trio dashed past them—two of them floating on air—they were convulsed with laughter. Uncle Guy would slap his thigh and his laughter would boom out. And Mother stood doubled up, holding her sides, which ached from laughing. A wave of humiliation and anger swept over Kittie. And each time the merry-go-round whirled them in view she grew more and more ashamed. Would the darn thing never stop! Everyone and everything seemed in league against them. But at last it came to a halt. Prince Charming helped his fair ladies to dismount, and without stopping to thank him, Kittie opened fire on her mother. "You said it would be all right for me to ride if someone asked me again. And then when I do what you say, you stand and make fun of me. I never want to see a merry-go-round again. So there!"

Mother and Uncle Guy tried to hide their amusement and Mother said, "Why, that was all right. I meant if a little boy asked you. I was just surprised to see you up there with Mr. Hall. But it's all right."

But Kittie's joy was dead now—she felt like a deflated balloon. And for a long, long time mention of the word "merry-go-round" brought back humiliating memories of that hateful ride. Have children ever really understood the words and actions of adults?

Mr. Hall was Roeser's hired man—thin, wiry, and small of feature and with very little above the collar. Harmless as a dove—gentle as a bar of ivory soap—but he had a weakness for little girls. Whenever they encountered him after that, the girls looked the other way—determined there would be no more invitations. Even the fireworks fell flat that evening after this disgusting episode.

One Sunday morning a few days after the Fourth of July Gertie picked up a torpedo that had been lying unnoticed on the ground on the north side of the house. It had been out in the rain and worthless, of course. She threw it against the house and wonder of wonders, it exploded with a loud bang. Astonished, the girls looked at each other wondering what their preacher grandfather would think of that—exploding a torpedo on Sunday! In later years they thought their anxiety had been unwarranted.

NOTES

Acker's Pine Grove was west of the Tittabawassee River. The wooden Freeland Road Bridge had been built in 1870 and was replaced with a steel bridge in 1895. The Lewis family would have traveled north to Freeland, crossed the bridge, and proceeded west. It may have been a large park area at Samuel P. Acker's 40-acre parcel located by the Guilford Drain and the Indian Reserve Line. It was also mentioned in Chapter 5.

Frank Lewis' store was on Main Street (Midland Road) near Washington Street. The vacant lot opposite might have been Noble King's parcel as shown on early maps. Freeland was a farming community. Hitching posts were placed in front of every business place. Whenever a circus came to town, a Fourth of July celebration, an election day, or another special event occurred, farm families came into the village. There were never enough hitching posts so the three church sheds were also used for horses and buggies. All the churches were near each other and in the center of the village's events.

Chapter 26

Christmas Shopping

Gertie and Kittie wanted to earn some money. Father gave them the job of cutting milkweeds in one of the fields. After several days of slashing, the milkweeds disappeared and the girls were paid 75 cents each. This money was deposited in their banks. Kittie's bank was a pink and gray elephant bank made of fine china. This money was to be invested in Christmas presents for the family and relatives.

Mrs. Eli Smith, our mailman's wife, lived in the house next to the present Haenke Apartments on Washington Street. In the front room she had a little gift shop with a few glass showcases. Her living quarters were behind this room. She could tell when customers came in by the tinkling of the little bell on the front door.

Mrs. Smith was a jolly, plump motherly sort of person—willing to wait indefinitely while juvenile customers made up their minds what they'd buy.

Spending all the afternoon dividing their purchases between her shop and Dietiker's Store they spent all the money, which they had pooled. They didn't consider buying anything for themselves. Their arithmetical ability being nothing to boast about, now and then they'd go out behind the store to count their money to see how many more gifts they could buy.

At day's end they had the beautiful dishes that would surprise and please the relatives: A big green glass sugar bowl with cover for Father (like the candy jars of later days); a pretty light blue translucent glass spoon holder for Mother (like a vase); a clear glass sugar and creamer for Aunts Ellen and Pollie; a matching one for Uncle Guy and Aunt Josie; green rose bowls with white flowers painted on the green glass for Aunt Mary and Uncle Herbert and their Sunday school teachers—Mrs. Nims and Mrs. Ella Olmsted (Ray's Mother).

This is a view of Washington Street looking west toward Midland Road. Gift shops or bazaars were the small stores that attracted Kittie and Gertie when they were doing their Christmas shopping. They shopped at Mrs. Smith's Store and Dietiker's Store for their pretty glass vases. Vasold Collection

Another year they weeded sugar beets for Uncle Guy and for Uncle Will for 50 cents a row—but those rows seemed endless, reaching almost to the woods. Uncle Guy paid promptly but they had quite a time getting paid by Uncle Will. Father got after him and finally the hard earned lucre was forthcoming.

On hands and knees the work of weeding and thinning was done with a little knife or hoe like tool. The rows were unending, and the hot sun beat down unmercifully on their young backs. Gertie was a good, fast worker. Louise did fairly well, too. But Kittie got so tired and couldn't keep up with them. So Gertie would come back and help her until she caught up with their rows. Over and over this procedure was repeated.

With sore hands and knees nearly raw, the last little beet had its life cut short as the end of the row was reached. That was the first, last, and only time the girls ever "signed a contract" to weed sugar beets.

That money furnished the where-with-all to buy the next Christmas

presents: A dark blue glass toothpick holder with three gold legs and gold trim around the top for Father; a beautiful yellow and white glass celery dish for Mother (to be used to stand celery up like flowers in a vase; with its fluted edge it makes a lovely vase today); lovely little vases all trimmed with gold with flowers painted on the front for Uncle Herbert and Aunt Mary and Uncle Guy and Aunt Josie. (Ina has the vase given to Uncle Herbert and Aunt Mary today.) All the relatives must have felt that Santa's pack that year was a veritable gold mine!

The best part of all this hard work and gift giving was the joy the girls experienced in giving to others. They truly learned the meaning of the Lord Jesus' words when He said in Acts 20:35—"*It is more blessed to give than to receive*."

Of course, the girls were given gifts by the relatives, in which probably more money but much less labor was involved.

My experience with little children in school the past few years when they were asked to tell about their Christmas was: "I got—and I got—" and on and on, but they seldom said "I gave." True joy comes from service and giving.

The German-American Sugar Company opened in Salzburg in 1901. It merged with the Robert Gage Coal Company in 1932, becoming the Monitor Sugar Company. The company is the largest sugar beet processing plant in the eastern states today. Freeland farmers hauled their sugar beets to this factory because it was closer to them. The farmer would take his loaded beet wagon to the factory at 5 or 6 A.M. and not return home until 5 or 6 P.M. Walter Thomson is the driver for Robert Law's beet wagon in 1909. Standing from left to right are Robert Law, George Manrel, and William Bishop. Vasold Collection

NOTES

Charles Dietiker served as the Postmaster from 1897 to 1908 and the Post Office was housed in his store on the southeast corner of Main and Washington Streets.

The sugar beet industry replaced Saginaw Valley's lumber industry in 1898 when Michigan Sugar Company built Michigan's first sugar factory in Essexville. The Bay City Sugar Company and West Bay City Sugar Company were built in 1899. In 1901 the German-American Sugar Company opened in Salzburg. It later became the Monitor Sugar Company. Because there was much competition between all the sugar companies, there was a great demand

Local farmers also hauled their sugar beets to the railroad weigh station during harvest time in October and November. These beets have been dumped at the Freeland Railroad Depot. Private residences are across from the holding ground on Depot Street. The beets would then be shipped by freight car to a sugar factory—either in Carrollton, Bay City, Salzburg, or Saginaw. Vasold Collection

for sugar beets. Farmers in Bay and Saginaw Counties raised sugar beets on their farms, and it provided a lucrative cash crop.

The multigerm sugar beet seed was imported from Germany until 1935. Because one seed ball produced six plants, it was necessary to manually block and thin out the five extra plants in early summer. When the beets were harvested in October, they were also manually topped (cut off the top) and then piled to be forked onto wagons. Horse drawn wagons hauled the beets to railroad stations or direct to the sugar factories for processing. Railroad stations delivered carloads of beets to the factory.

A farmer was only able to raise a few acres of beets because everything was done manually. Usually the entire family worked in the beet fields during the growing and harvest season. Or, young boys would be hired to help out. Mexican migrant laborers also worked in Bay-Saginaw beet fields. After World War II the entire industry became refined and mechanized. Bay-Saginaw Valley is known as Michigan's Sugar Bowl, and the sugar beet industry remains a major Michigan agricultural industry today.

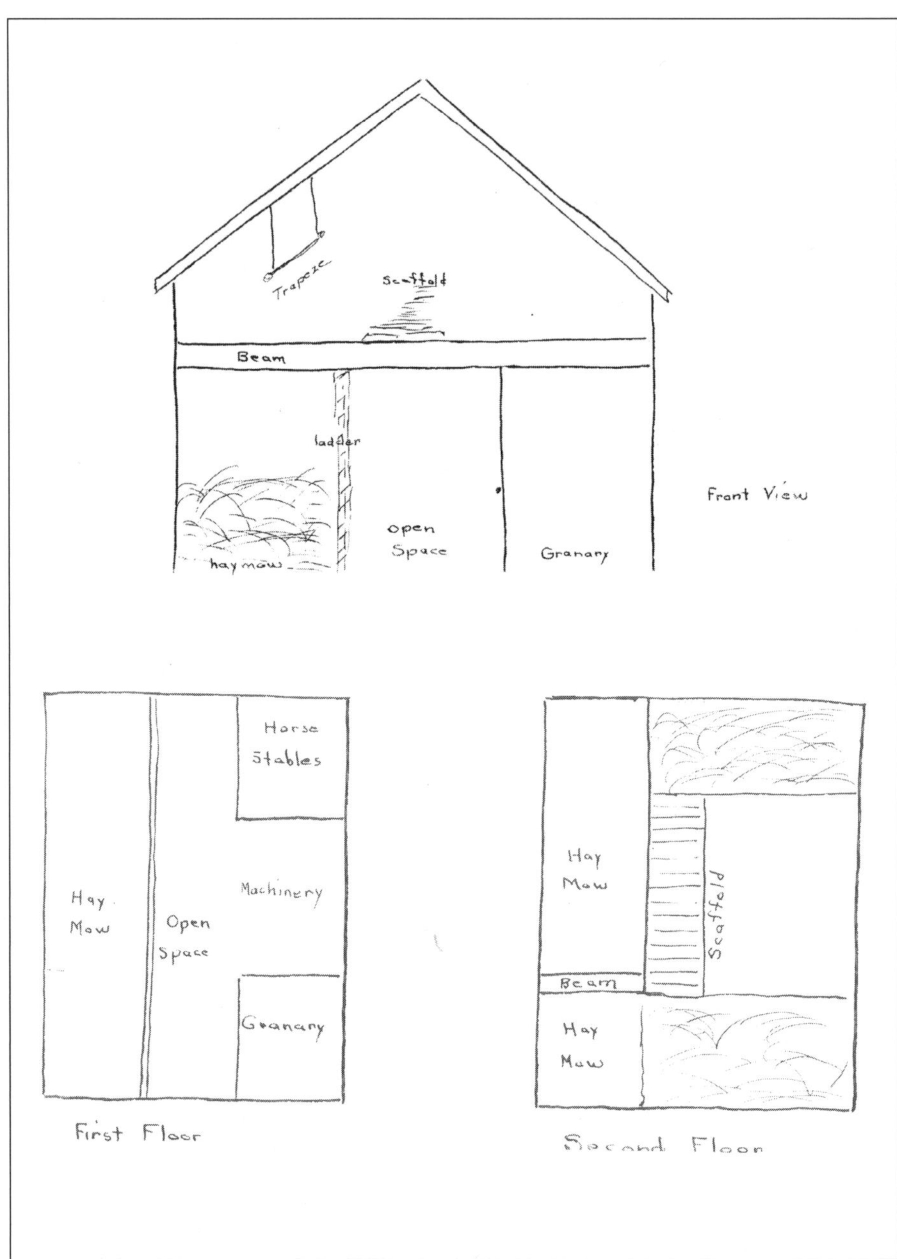
Trapeze
Scaffold
Beam
ladder
Front View
open Space
Granary
haymow
Horse Stables
Hay Mow
Open Space
Machinery
Granary
First Floor
Hay Mow
Scaffold
Beam
Hay Mow
Second Floor

Chapter 27

Fun and Tragedy in the Barns

Across the side road (Pierce Road) on Grandpa Lewis' farm were two big barns, which were designated "The Barn" and "The Farther Barn." The Barn was nearer and the one usually chosen to play in. It contained the horse stables enclosed at the east corner of the north end over which was a floor where hay could be stored and pitched down for feed and bedding for the horses.

In the east corner of the south end was a granary where the threshed wheat and oats were stored in large bins. This, too, was a room enclosed. It was a common occurrence for the girls to climb into a bin, sit there and eat the grains of wheat unaware that Vitamin B was stored there in abundance. Vitamins were an unknown quantity in the '90's but grains of wheat were a toothsome morsel. It mattered little if mice got in the bins, too, provided their visit didn't coincide with that of the girls.

Pieces of farm machinery were stored between the horse stables and the granary: Harvester (binder) machine, mowing machine, corn planter, plow, and spike-toothed drag. Many of these were equipped with sharp cutting knives.

The entire west side of the barn was a haymow, and the center section was vacant space for traveling through with the horses, etc. Above this vacant space was a scaffold extending from the ceiling of the stables to the floor above the granary and south central part of the barn. This scaffold was like a walk four or five feet wide several feet high. One side of it was about even with the front of the haymow.

At the end of haying season the mow was filled with hay almost to the eaves. But as the year wore on, it became lower and lower, leaving it a long way down from the scaffold.

When hay was high in the mow Floyd had succeeded in getting a trapeze fastened to the rafters under the steep roof. His chums from the Freeland School were drawn to this trapeze as moths to a street light or flies to a honey pot. They spent many happy hours doing stunts and tricks there—Fred Branch, Bert Preston, Barney Haviland, etc.

When Gertie and Kittie tried to follow them, Fred would say, "Floyd, I wouldn't have those little pests following me."

When Floyd began working on the railroad, the old trapeze was almost abandoned. But an attraction with a danger tag attached couldn't possibly stay abandoned. The girls and their chums began making use of it—unknown to their parents: Meta Cubbage, Murl Freeland, Lula Haviland, Louise, and others.

If getting from the scaffold to the trapeze was a ticklish job, jumping backwards from the trapeze to the scaffold was ticklish to the nth degree! Gertie was big enough to jump out and grab on the trapeze, but Kittie was too little for that. Gertie and Louise used to pull the trapeze back with the pitchfork, and then hold her up where she could reach it.

Ignorance was bliss! They all became adept at this and gradually could hang by their knees, swinging back and forth in an upside down world—pulling themselves back up before jumping into the hay. But they preferred jumping backwards to the scaffold because this eliminated that steep climb up the ladder to get back up from the main floor.

Mother's hair would have turned gray overnight and Father would have been bald long before he was had they known how their darlings were occupied in the barn.

Willie Cubbage used to pasture their cow on the Haines place, and on the way back often stopped and asked for a d-d-dill p-p-p-pickle and incidentally to inquire if he could p-p-p-play w-w-with the g-g-g-girls. Mother's consent was always forthcoming. Playing "Bear" was a favorite sport. Willie, as the Bear, was chasing the three girls up the ladder, over the huge square beams, across the scaffold and back again. Just as Kittie jumped from the beam into the haymow, Willie swung out on the trapeze—his knees striking her in the side knocking her breath completely out. Her eyes grew big and frightened as she tried to speak but couldn't say a word. She had a painful ache in the region of her stomach

and things grew dark as she began to black out. Gertie and Louise carried her to the main floor and laid her on a wagon seat that was standing there.

Willie, cringing with fear that he had killed her, hid behind a box or something with just his bulging eyes peering over to watch her breathe her last. Finally Mother was called and she came on the run. Mother began to rub her, but Kittie began to breathe again and soon was her normal self again. A flood of relief and joy spread over Willie's face as he realized that prison bars were not in the offing for him this time.

But the following day was a tragic one in the life of the girls. There where their beloved trapeze had hung was just an empty space. Father had cut the Gordian knot and the trapeze became only a precious memory relegated to the past.

Many of their happiest play experiences took place in the barn. No matter how occupied they were with their play they always heard Albert Dietiker's light wagon when it stopped at the gate. He and Charlie Dietiker operated a general store. And Albert would stock his light wagon with soap, sugar, bright shiny pans, etc. and travel through the countryside to increase their sales. The girls knew that somewhere in that wagon was a little tin pail filled with hard candy used for treats for children when a purchase was made. Their sixth sense always told them when that wagon stopped at the gate. They'd file out of the barn and start to the house as though they didn't know he was there. While

Mother looked over the wares, three pairs of hungry-for-sweets eyes were looking wistfully for that candy pail. Mr. Dietiker would bring it to light and put a few pieces in the extended dirty hands. And Mother would have some new supplies for her larder. Service with a smile—and a fistful of candy in the bargain.

With the trapeze gone, Kittie had to think of something new. Ah, she'd surprise the girls! Going to the barn alone she climbed up on the beam and stood looking down into the mow. Getting up her courage she leaped into the air, turning a complete somersault on the way down. That was fun! She did this several times. Then wanting an audience she called the girls to watch her aerial act. Feeling very smart and cocky she climbed the ladder and walked out on the beam. In her hurry to show off she jumped into space but didn't turn quite soon enough. Down she came landing on her shoulders instead of her feet. The girls rubbed her neck and shoulders for a few minutes. Then undaunted she tried it again, making a perfect landing. She was a heroine now!

In the barnyard of "The Farther Barn" was an old sheep—a ram. He was rather cross. Being chased by this ram was a favorite sport of the girls. They would stand between him and the barn door. They'd take a few steps toward him and stamp a foot. He'd take a few steps toward them and stamp his front hoof. This was repeated until not too much space was between the girls and the ram. His white eyes had a wicked gleam in them and as the girls whirled and ran into the barn, he was hot on their trail. And just as they threw themselves over the manger wall, his hard head hit the manger with a resounding whack. This was repeated over and over to the girls' enjoyment. The ram seemed to get some fun out of it, too. At any rate, he was never loath to enter into the game.

After the girls had seen the Saginaw Bay Louise and Kittie would take their dolls to the barn, pretending the hay was water. Undressing their dolls they would put on imaginary bathing suits and go in the water with them.

The Haines barn also furnished a place for play. It had massive timbers and beams but no hay. There was an old red light wagon behind the barn. One day the girls wheeled it to the top of the hill and holding the fills up in the air rode down the hill, which was fairly steep. Mother shuddered when she heard about this long afterward. Looking back through those years, Kittie knew now that the girls' guardian angels must have been kept busy watching over them.

NOTES

Dietiker's Store was one of Freeland's largest general stores. It was common practice in rural communities for the general store's owner to stock his delivery wagon or van with basic essentials and call upon housewives throughout the rural area. Transportation was difficult, if not impossible, and women would not always have the time or means to visit the store in town. Besides, housewives were busy from morning to night with manual labor in the cooking, cleaning, food preservation, and laundry. They had very little time for themselves.

Chapter 28

The Manure Wagon

Gertie and Kittie were the proud owners of a little red wagon known as an Express Wagon. They often used it on the farm as they saw their father use the big wagon. A wagon was used for many purposes. For hauling oats, wheat, beans, or hay Father would put the hayrack on the wagon. This widened the wagon top considerably making it possible to spread the load evenly, and it could be piled much higher.

For spreading manure the wagon box was removed and long, loose boards were laid lengthwise on the frame, a wide board on each side held in place by stakes pushed through a ring or gadget on each side. Manure could not be placed way to the end of the boards, or the jolting of the wagon would have shaken it off. So the last two or three feet were left empty with the ends acting like a springboard.

It was a Red Letter Day for the three girls when they saw Father getting the manure wagon ready. It must have seemed more like a Brown Letter Day to Mother when she saw the color of their dresses and underclothes after several rides on the spring boards. They always climbed up and sat on the ends of those floppy boards on the way to the field, springing up and down in glee as they rode. Upon reaching the field they'd jump off. The manure was pitched to the ground with a pitchfork. And when the load was emptied Father would loosen the stakes, letting the sideboards down—the manure side face down on the other dirty boards.

Then the girls had to sit sideways on these sideboards as they rode back to the barnyard for another load. This was one of their favorite sports. They loved the smell as well as the ride. Their clothes looked as though they had wallowed in tobacco juice, and even their hindends were stained yellow. But Mother didn't care—she believed in letting them have a good time.

Regardless of how busy they were at other play, that manure wagon never got away from the barnyard without three little tomboys on the end boards. In after years the sight or smell of a barnyard made them nostalgic!

CHAPTER 29

THE CIRCUS

Sensational news! A tent circus coming to Freeland! Attractions of this nature were as rare as a swimming pool in the desert, and appealed to old and young alike. A nominal fee would admit the entire family. At that time Barnum & Bailey wasn't a familiar name in the girls' vocabulary. So the children with wonder and admiration viewed every act of that 2 x 2 circus. The trained dog acts; the clowns; the acrobats—all were breathtaking! But when Beulah came out for her trapeze act, the kids went wild. Beulah with the pretty blonde curls and big blue eyes! She cupped her pretty white hands, turned the palms outward at the sides of her face, made a graceful courtesy and climbed into the trapeze.

For the next few minutes Beulah had the children in the land of enchantment. She was encored several times. Then, again cupping her hands and bringing them forward in a sweeping motion, which included her worshipful young audience, she disappeared into her dressing tent amid the deafening applause.

At least two of the children walked away from that circus with the determination to embark on a new career—Louise and Kittie would be joining a circus!

The next day to the delight and surprise of all the children, Beulah appeared at school. She sat with some of the town girls and was surrounded by a bevy of worshipful female admirers. In fact, those admirers were envious. No Queen for a Day on Jim Bailey's TV show ever received more sincere plaudits than did our lovely little Beulah. Though Louise and Kittie were compelled to admit that in the bright daylight minus grease paint, eye shadow, and other circus paraphernalia, Beulah looked a little less alluring.

For several days play took on a new nature as the girls did daring feats on the trapeze with only the barn roof for the big top and an imaginary audience seated on the scaffold and in the haymow. This continued until new interests vied with the circus and Beulah became only a pleasant memory—a symbol of the circus!

NOTES

Several circuses came to Michigan throughout the summer months. Because they traveled by train, the circuses would have made a stopover in Freeland since the Flint & Pere Marquette Railroad passed through town. Two or three or four circuses might come to Saginaw during the summer months. Some of them would also go through small towns on their way to larger towns such as Midland or Bay City. The circus was a great attraction for both young and old. Usually there was a free street parade to advertise for their following tent show. Admittance was charged for the tent show. This was a source of great entertainment to the town folks, and families would come from miles around to see the circus. Also, the circus bought provisions and animal feed from towns along their route. The circus would have helped Freeland's economy.

Chapter 30

Playhouses

Playing house was a favorite pastime of the girls. The abandoned Haines house across the road made a very good playhouse. At first, the three girls played downstairs, each girl choosing one of the three rooms for her house. Later on, they conceived the idea of playing upstairs which was reached by a rickety, winding stairway. They must have a stove as all children love to cook. But the only available one was the old, old cook stove in the lean-to kitchen, which was in a dilapidated condition.

Moving at a snail's pace they succeeded in reaching the stairway after alternate periods of carrying and resting, carrying and resting. How to get that heavy iron appliance up the stairs was the problem. Gertie went first, backing up the stairs and hanging on the front. Kittie was on the side, and Louise was at the most dangerous place—at the foot where a miscalculation or a misstep could have avalanched that heavy cast iron stove directly upon her.

Inching along one step and resting, one step at a time—after what seemed hours of strenuous effort they succeeded in making the last step, setting the stove on firm footing upstairs. By the time it was settled in a satisfactory spot, blue and purple welts showed on their hands. But it gave them a feeling of satisfaction and accomplishment.

Another day they found a part of a log down by the Tittabawassee River, and by the same laborious method carried it up the steep hill and up the stairs—transforming it into a couch or sofa.

The house boasted an old bed frame—just headboard, footboard, and two sideboards minus slats, springs, and mattress. This was set up in the bedroom end of the big room. Somewhere they found a piece of yellow crockery (just the

bottom piece) and deposited it in the customary place—under the bed. More and more the place acquired a homelike atmosphere. And happy play went on day after day.

One morning when Willie Cubbage had turned his cow into the pasture he stopped at the house to get some more d-d-dill p-p-p-pickles. Poor Willie was a confirmed stutterer. His steps were heard on the stairway and he could see at a glance that all that was lacking was a father to the family. Gertie was mother and Louise and Kittie the children.

Bedtime came and the three girls climbed into bed over the sideboards and lay down on the floor, imagining they were in bed. It seemed so real to Willie, who was a few months younger than Kittie, that he reached under the bed and produced the yellow crockery saying, "Well, I guess this is the last thing before going to bed." And to the horror and chagrin of the rest of the family he suited his actions to his words, leaving a trickle of a golden trail running over the bedroom floor.

All the girls had been taught modesty to the nth degree, so they expressed their disapproval and the family relationship broke up then and there. Willie was embarrassed and soon left for home. The girls decided it was more fun keeping house without a husband and father. Thereafter, when Willie came their play took the form of running games to divert his mind from becoming too realistic.

Another favorite spot was under a big cottonwood tree in the little gully between their house and Louise's. They worked a long time making and setting up an R.F.D. mailbox outside the fence near the road. It had a flag that could be raised and lowered. Mr. Eli Smith was their mail carrier at the time and was quite amused at their efforts, so occasionally he'd drop something in the box to their delight.

Grandpa Lewis liked to surprise them by "mailing" little books to them as he walked down the road to Aunt Mary's. They acquired such books as: *Lucy At The Seashore, Lucy At The Mountains, The Carrier Pigeon, Little Ferns For Fanny's Little Friends, A Child's Repentance,* etc. Some were of 1834 vintage, which had been given to the Jaquith girls by their mother when they were little girls. In this way they built up a little library.

An old bachelor, Mr. McCarty, lived about five miles down the road toward Saginaw. Once in awhile when he'd drive by on the way from Freeland, he'd leave a sack of candy in the mailbox.

Uncle Guy and Charlie and Guy Foote used to slip some candy in, too. All in all they did a thriving business in that amateur mailbox. Needless to say the girls didn't realize they were defrauding Uncle Sam by sending and receiving mail without the required postage.

Quite a distance from the house at the south end of the garden was the site of another playhouse. This was settled during the canning season. Most summer foods were preserved for winter use by canning. The girls had seen their mother can pears, plums, peaches, tomatoes, ketchup, chili sauce, etc. in one and two quart cans. They went through the fields gathering milkweed pods, seeds, plantain and what have you. They even used soil and chunks of clay. These were mixed with water and poured into glass bottles by the dozen. In later years the girls were filled with remorse to think they had even filled the large Blue Willow Ware sugar bowl, which had belonged to their Grandma Allen and made in Hindustani—a real antique. True, it had lost both of its handles, but still would have been worthy to grace the corner whatnot as a hand-me-down antique—a family heirloom!

A cellar was dug in the ground and all the canned goods were stored there and covered for the winter. But alas! Winter had taken a heavy toll. The shallow cellar was above frost line and spring revealed every bottle and container with their seams burst and their "innards" oozing out the cracks. Chili sauce, mincemeat, plums—all united their flavors and identified themselves with the broken rubble of the shallow cellar. The Blue Willow Ware found itself thrown on the junk pile with the various strata of society—broken crocks, dishes, bottles, leaky old pans, etc. Another play activity was abandoned as young minds were gradually gaining wisdom from their many experiments and experiences. How true the maxim: "Learn to do by doing."

On various Christmases Kittie had asked for and received a cupboard full of dishes (see the china cabinet for these dishes—that is, the ones left after five of her young nieces played with them); a doll bed; a doll chair; a little brass oil lamp; and a three-piece china tea set. Father made the girls a sturdy table. So on rainy days and in winter they could set up housekeeping any day in the house—usually in the bedroom.

The Christmas Kittie was seven years old (1898) her parents gave her that three-piece lovely Bavarian china tea set. All her milk and water had to be poured from this teapot for a long time. She drank quarts of water and almost became waterlogged. And in later years Kittie marveled that she didn't die from internal drowning—as she read in the *News* that one little girl actually died from internal drowning because she drank so much water from her play dishes.

The cupboard with dishes came when she was nine years old (1900). She had asked for dishes and Gertie, for a ring—which was yellow gold with turquoise "sets." Kittie was so domestic in her tastes that everyone thought she'd be the one to settle down as a housewife. Gertie was always a "maid" teaching school, much preferring that to housekeeping. But in later years the tables were turned—Gertie became the housewife, Kittie the teacher, and each was happy in her chosen sphere.

One summer Arthur Lewis came to visit and stayed a month. He was about fifteen months older than Kittie and she was in seventh heaven. She could never get enough running. Gertie would play running games for a while but soon tired of them, and when it was her turn to be "IT" she was ready to quit or to play something else. So Kittie would say, ""Oh, well, if you'll play again I'll be It." Anything to prolong the game! But with a strong healthy boy around, she could run to her heart's content.

Floyd was so much older that she had always wanted a younger brother. So Arthur and the three girls had a wonderful summer.

One evening while sitting at the play table near the window in Mother's bedroom, Arthur had a bright idea. In the center of the table was that little brass oil lamp with its thin fluted brass shade. Arthur held a celluloid comb over the chimney. Celluloid is highly inflammable and soon the comb was ablaze, igniting the window curtain. In terror the girls looked at Arthur, and he looked at them. All seemed to go into shock. As though hypnotized, they kept mum.

Mother must have had her weather eye open toward the bedroom, for out of the tail of her eye she saw the blaze and extinguished it before any damage was done—except to a corner of the curtain. No one appeared to know how that curtain caught fire. Arthur's bright idea had materialized in a brighter manner than he had expected. Another scientific experiment tried, even though the solution wasn't quite clear. "Why did the comb burn?" they wondered. As for Mother, she decided that their play activities merited closer scrutiny in the future—at least, while Arthur was with them.

It was a lonesome Kittie when Arthur's mother and father came from Unionville to take him home at the end of the summer. Mother was glad there was no younger brother in the family to think up any new mischief.

These various playhouses show how the girls were trying to interpret through their many experiences the adult life in their own environment as seen through their eyes.

NOTES

The Haines house was directly across the road from the Lewis farm. This is also the house in which Kittie was born in 1891. Grandpa Lewis' second wife was Aurora Jaquith. Therefore, he would have had the childhood books that Aurora had used, and he passed them on to his granddaughters. Charles Foote had a farm adjacent to Jacob Lewis. He was a neighbor and would have driven by the Lewis farm and the girls' mailbox. Arthur Lewis was the girls' first cousin and was the son of William Lewis. This Lewis family lived in Unionville. They were discussed in Chapter 10.

This two-story Freeland School District #3 building was built in 1872 on the northeast corner of Church & Second Streets. The Adventist Church was across Second Street on the northwest corner as shown on the left side of the photo. The Congregational Church was behind the school on Third Street. This is the school that Floyd, Gertie, and Kittie attended for grades one through ten, walking to and from school daily. Olmsted Family Collection

Chapter 31

School Play

For several years the Freeland School had only two rooms. Upstairs was a large room used for entertainments and for a lodge room. Often at noon some of the children ate their lunches while sitting on the stairway. At the top of the long stairs was a locked door. Sometimes there was such a terrible smell coming from behind that door. Someone said a goat was kept up there for joiners to ride when being initiated into the lodge. Kittie had never seen a goat so she could readily believe one might have that disagreeable smell.

The girls would wonder—what would happen if that goat broke through the door? It made the hair on Kittie's arms stand up straight thinking about it. But she also thought it might be fun for they could run (something she never tired of) and the goat could chase them. But it must have been anchored firmly up there as it never made its appearance. They learned later that the lodge kept Limburger cheese for their initiation ceremonies.

For some time only the two lower rooms were used in the frame building. They were designated as primary and grammar rooms. In later years all three rooms were used for classrooms. Students were seated at stationary double desks and the teacher's desk was on a raised platform. A big stove stoked with coal stood in the center of the room and there were three heat zones: Frigid, Temperate and Torrid—depending upon how far or near one sat from the stove. Later a jacket was built around the stove for better circulation of heat.

A water pail and dipper stood on a shelf or bench in the hall. On extremely hot days two boys were allowed to pass the water pail around so each child could quench his thirst.

A large bell hung in the belfry and the teacher rang it several times each day: First bell at 8:30 A.M.; then at 9:00 A.M. when the session began. Recess came at 10:30—the bell rang at 10:45. The afternoon session began at 1:00 P.M. so the bell was rung a few minutes before 1:00 and then again at 1:00 o'clock. The afternoon recess was at 2:30 and the bell called the children back in at 2:45 P.M.

Outdoor plumbing was the only kind of plumbing in those days. Two outhouses or toilets stood near the east end of the lot with board sidewalks leading to them.

Louise and Kittie each bought a doll at Dietiker's store for 15 cents. It had a china head with black hair painted on, china hands and shoes, and a pink cloth body stuffed with sawdust. It was terribly out of proportion, long-geared, and very thin with tiny hands and feet. They carried their dolls to school in their pockets, letting them sit between them during school hours. Then at noon they sewed for them—if you could call it that. Kittie never could handle a needle and thread, so she just cut a hole big enough to fit over the head and ran a puckering string through to keep it from slipping off. A few long stitches to keep the sides together and the doll had a new dress.

Other days children lined up on the stairs and slid down the long slippery banisters. This was almost as much fun as riding on a merry-go-round. At first a big girl stood at the bottom to catch the small fry before they went whooshing off on the floor. But they soon grew adept at stopping at just the right moment. Day after day that old banister grew smoother and smoother, preventing their seats from getting slivers or callouses. This was the forerunner of the present-day playground slide!

Then, again, the girls would gather twigs and sticks and make playhouses the entire length of the playground by sticking them close together in the ground to outline the various rooms. It seemed a dumb play but they thought it was fun.

A favorite circle game was "Lose your supper." A runner ran around the circle touching someone on the back who then ran in the opposite direction trying to get back to starting place first. The loser "lost his supper" and became "IT" for the next game.

One day just as Jennie King ran around and jumped into the vacant place her petticoat fell off. "Ha, ha, ha," shouted the boys. "Jennie lost more

than her supper that time!" But Jennie nonchalantly picked it up, ran over and tucked it under the high boardwalk leading to the girls' outhouse (cat house, the boys called it) and the game continued.

Another favorite sport was jumping the rope. This involved teamwork. Six girls with three long ropes lined up a few feet apart. The rest of the girls lined up in a single line facing the ropes. The object was to see if each girl could run and jump over each rope as it was being turned without missing. It really took some skill to synchronize one's running and jumping with that of the revolving ropes, but there were some girls that could do it. This gave each one plenty of exercise and was lots of fun.

The big boys used to chase the big girls around the room at noon. One noon just as Kittie put her thumb on the door latch to go outdoors Pearl Howd ran from the big (grammar) room through the little (primary) room with Floyd in hot chase. He opened the door pinching Kittie's thumb in the latch and raced pell-mell to catch his prey, unaware that he had hurt her. That nail turned black and blue and green and after several days came off, leaving a tender, new nail in its place.

The school stood between the Congregational Church sheds on the north and the Adventist Church sheds on the west. These were ideal places for hide-and-seek. Boys and girls of all ages entered into the game, often sliding through a little opening in the back to get in "free."

By the Congregational sheds was a pile of heavy lumber, which made very satisfactory teeterboards over the partitions between the horse stalls. Noon times and recesses were never dull because they were totally unsupervised! Teachers took these periods, not for coffee breaks or for smoking, but for a break in the monotony of hearing recitations and disciplining unruly students. Sometimes they went to their boarding houses for lunch—then Old Ned was to pay. Students were free to choose and pursue their favorite games and activities. Big girls jumped over broomsticks held higher and higher with more than one broomstick being broken. Gertie and Winnie Stolze were the champion high jumpers.

Glenn Branch one noon let himself out the upstairs window, which was very high in that old building. Then he found he couldn't pull himself back in. He pleaded and begged for help and Herb Olmsted and Marshall Freeland pulled him back in, a frightened but wiser boy.

If things got too dull it was a simple matter to get an afternoon off. All the boys had to do was to stoke the old pot-bellied stove with an extra generous amount of coal, leave the stove door open, and soon the smoke-filled room made the afternoon session impossible. When Mrs. Meredith came back at noon the stove door was closed and students stood with worried faces—their eyes and throats smarting. "The stove has been smoking just something awful," someone would say and school was dismissed for the rest of the day. The school board director was notified that the stove needed cleaning. This was just as big a boon then as when ice-coated highways and drifted snow close schools today. Probably more so then because of the mystery element!

Being dismissed early gave country children an opportunity to go downtown before going home.

Mrs. Meredith began reading the *Horatio Alger* books aloud in the afternoon. The students sat fascinated and spellbound. The way in which his heroes rose from poverty and obscurity and climbed the ladder of financial success—leaping from rung to rung made the girls wish they had been born males so they could have done some heroic deeds and won fame and fortune.

Mrs. Wiggs of the *Cabbage Patch* by Kate Douglas Wiggins was another favorite. The ingenuity of Mrs. Wiggs in raising her large family in respectability without much means set the listeners in gales of laughter, and sometimes Mrs. Meredith had difficulty in reading some of the passages as she, too, was convulsed with the humorous incidents.

Other favorites were Peck's *Bad Boy* and Toby Tyler of the *Circus*. All looked forward to that time of day when lessons could be put aside and each

When dismissed from school early, the girls walked to Washington Street and watched the blacksmith at work at Preston's Village Blacksmith Shop. Horses were the main means of travel so several blacksmith shops were needed to keep horse hooves trimmed and shoed. This is the Claude Rix Blacksmith Shop. Dr. Ostrander is leaning against the door. The sidewalk is made of pine planks, and the road is a dirt or mud highway. Vasold Collection

one could enter the enchanted land of imagination in Story Land.

After Kittie had taken some music lessons she became the school organist accompanying the whole group in such songs as: *The Glad May Morn, Happy Greeting To All, Johnny McCree, Would You Like To Know, Kind Words, Tick! Said The Clock, The Bird With A Broken Pinion,* etc. and many good rounds. On Murl's last day at school, October 14, 1904, before moving to California they sang at her request: #221 *The Cottage On The Hill* and #159 *Far Away.* And that was a sad time for the children as it seemed farther away at that time than does the Middle and Far East today.

Herb Olmsted began asking Kittie to play some songs during the noon hour, and he stood by the organ and turned the music for her. She was always ready to play when anyone asked her and she was rather flattered as Herb was three years and a few months older than she. For the rest of that school year they were very much in love with each other so she was more than glad to oblige him. She could hardly wait until the next day when she could play for him again. That was eleven-year-old puppy love! A perfectly grand feeling!

When school was dismissed early the girls would go downtown. How they loved to loiter in front of Preston's Village Blacksmith Shop. They watched the bellows make the fire burn brighter where he heated the iron. And then they could hear his hammer's blows on the anvil where he shaped the shoes for the horses. As he pounded the red-hot iron the sparks flew this way and that way. Then to watch him pick up the horse's foot and holding it against his leather apron nail the shoe in place while Old Dobbin stood waiting patiently. Children never tired of watching this operation. Country roads were very icy in winter, and without shoes horses were in danger of falling.

Then, too, the girls would have time to go to the stores. If they were lucky enough to have a penny in their pockets, they could buy a stick of white lady gum with a ring to be worn on a finger. Imagine! All of this for a penny! Those good old days! There were the Munger and Lewis Stores on Main Street, Dietiker's on Washington & Main Streets, and Howd's at Washington & Depot Streets. At Mrs. Eli Smith's gift shop in her home's front room on Washington Street the girls could buy pretty colored glass dishes, tiny pocketbooks, tiny dolls, etc. ranging in price from 5 to 25 cents.

At one time it became popular for one school to visit another school in winter—an excuse for getting a sleigh ride! One day the teacher and students were packed into three or four sleighs and they visited the Wiltse School, which was on a very winding road. One horse fell on the ice and bled a little at the nose. The girls felt so sorry for the horse. Accustomed to farm animals, as they were—to them animals seemed like people. From there they went on and visited the LaPorte School, which consisted of two rooms. By a sliding partition or some such arrangement the two rooms were thrown into one and an impromptu program given by participants of each school. One older girl sang *Poor Peggy* with an echo effect with Dolly Winslow at the organ. Future citizens of LaPorte and Freeland mingled their youthful voices in such songs

Delos H. Howd operated this General Store from 1891 to 1903 at Washington & Depot Streets. He carried groceries, dry goods, shoes, and furniture. The Freeland Elevator is seen in the background. The sidewalks are pine planked. Hitching posts line the store's side. Vasold Collection

as: *Ko Ka Cha Lunk Cha Lunk Cha Leigh Li, Twenty Froggies Went To School, Tenting On The Old Camp Ground, Whistle And Hoe,* etc. from the old familiar *Knapsack.*

Mrs. Freeland told Mother to let the girls stay with Murl any night as Murl was at their house so often. So once in awhile they found it a real treat. Mrs. Freeland was never quite sure what she'd have for supper until Mr. Freeland came home from the Shop. He was a very good barber and did a little jeweler work as a sideline. He was a good provider and usually brought good beefsteak when he came home at night; and Bertie, the older daughter who clerked in a store, brought bread and cookies, etc. And oh, what a treat store bread was! And those Mary Ann cookies! On the whole the girls preferred their mother's good home baking. But "Variety is the spice of life," so the change was welcomed occasionally.

Beefsteak was a real treat as Father didn't raise cattle for market and never

This two-story, four-room brick North Building was built in 1914 and replaced the frame school building. The Odd Fellows purchased the frame school and used it for their lodge meetings until 1953. When Kittie began teaching in the Freeland Primary Department in 1919, she taught in this building. When fire destroyed part of the building, Kittie and the other teachers taught in the next-door Congregational Church until it was rebuilt. The North Building was demolished in 1974. Vasold Collection

butchered the calves. Murl was as carefree as Gertie and Kittie and with supper over, was free to play. Bertie was a lovely young lady, so kind and thoughtful of her mother.

Hide-and-seek in the Adventist Church sheds was the typical play. All the neighborhood kids congregated in the sheds—a strange conglomeration ranging in ages from seven to fifteen or more: The twins—Victor and Vernor Freeland, Murl, Gertie, Kittie, Meta, Willie and Max Cubbage, Lula Haviland, Earl Dietiker, Norman Brown and Ross Dunn. Age barriers were wiped out as "IT" was pursuing the elusive hiders while some were coming in "free" through the gap in the back wall where a board was missing.

Darkness sent the hiders and seekers to their various homes for the night. Then the Freeland house became a bears' den with Victor and Vernor's chasing the girls behind furniture, under the bed, and every other imaginable place.

The Arthur Hill High School,
Saginaw, W. S., Mich.
219856

After an addition was made to this West Side High School in 1901, it was renamed the Arthur Hill High School. It was located at southeast Court & Harrison Streets directly across from First Presbyterian Church. The Freeland School ended with the tenth grade. Kittie attended Arthur Hill High School for her eleventh and twelfth grades, graduating in 1909. Having just been renovated, Arthur Hill would have been a very modern school during her years there. Ederer Collection

For once Kittie could get enough running. Mrs. Freeland laughed and never interfered with their play, not even the time they tipped over the customary piece of china under the bed, sending its contents hither and yon! Then came bedtime with three in a bed where talk continued far into the night.

What a change to leave school for lunch—mostly sandwiches and cookies, and not so much time for the usual noon activities. At the end of another school day the overnighters were overjoyed to roost in their own nest again.

NOTES

There were four schools in Tittabawassee Township before the Civil War (1861-1865). These were the Freeland, Munger, Vasold, and Wellman Schools. The two-story Freeland School District #3 building was built in 1872 and served the community until the two-story four room brick North Building was built in 1914. The Odd Fellows purchased the old school and used it for their lodge hall until 1953. It was then demolished and the present Township Office and Fire Department were built on the site. The present Township parking lot was the Congregational Church site.

The Wiltse School was located in Thomastown Township just past Tittabawassee Road on the west side of the Tittabawassee River. The LaPorte School was located in Midland County south of Freeland and north of Hemlock. The two schools would have been somewhat close to each other.

Kittie attended the two-story frame schoolhouse for ten years until about 1907 and then finished high school at Arthur Hill High School in Saginaw, graduating about 1909. She attended the first Arthur Hill High School located on the southeast corner of Harrison & Court Streets directly across from First Presbyterian Church. Arthur Hill moved to its present site on Mackinaw Street in 1940.

Chapter 32

Cousin Hazel's Visit

Mother's brother, Uncle John Allen, used to brag a great deal about his youngest daughter, Hazel (Sawdon). And when Uncle Guy came home after visiting relatives in Grand Ledge, all he could talk about was Hazel. She was a wonder—a brilliant girl! What she didn't know wasn't worth knowing. She was a tall young lady, so grown-up, etc. For no reason whatever the girls began to dislike her. They couldn't bear to see Uncle Guy's affection transferred to a cousin that they didn't even know.

Then one day the bomb shell exploded by way of a letter stating that Hazel was coming for a two-week visit. Faces fell and gloom polluted the atmosphere. Now they'd have to give up their tomboy play and be quiet and ladylike. They couldn't go barefooted. They couldn't play in the barn! They couldn't ride on the manure wagon. They couldn't do this and they couldn't do that. They'd have to be dressed up. Why did unknown cousins have to visit anyway? Summer vacation with no fun was almost tragic!

On the designated date Cousin Hazel arrived. Although a month younger than Gertie she was head and shoulders above her. She made Louise and Kittie look like pygmies. She certainly looked the part! The girls were filled with awe.

Hazel changed her traveling clothes to everyday clothes and suggested they go barefooted. The girls were goggle eyed. Did she say barefooted? Off with shoes and stockings and the next minute they were out on the muddy road with the mud squishing, oozing between their toes. Hazel was going to be fun! She loved our barn. She loved our river. Above all she loved the old cart.

Uncle Guy invited several girls there one afternoon to a party in her honor.

They played games in the parlor and one game in particular made a lot of fun. All the girls were seated on chairs with legs crossed. Murl, too, was seated sitting on one leg; and over her other leg and tucked under her dress was her stocking stuffed to look like her leg.

Uncle Guy was summoned from the other room and told to go around the circle giving a good hard pull to each girl's right leg. He, good old scout that he was, was always ready for anything. He had gone past three or four girls, pulling their legs but couldn't quite see the object of the game. Then Murl's turn came. She was a big strong girl and he gave her an extra hard jerk and off came her leg high in the air. He was flabbergasted, thinking he had maimed her for life.

When undergoing any surprise or any unusual exertion he always had a habit of puffing—not quite as loudly as the old wolf, but a very noticeable puffing. There he stood with Murl's severed leg up in the air, puffing and saying, "Why! Why!" His face was covered with surprise and chagrin as he saw Murl's leg dangling there. Shrieks of laughter filled the room and the younger fry thought that Uncle Guy really was terrified. Then his hearty laugh boomed out, drowning out the others. Everyone voted him a good sport.

Gertie told Uncle Guy to open and shut his hand several times making a good fist. After he did this, she said, "You'd make a good lemon squeezer!" Of course, this tickled him. Later on she said, "That's one on you." He bit and said, "What?" "A dirty shirt," she answered. You see, gags were common even then.

Later in the afternoon they all enjoyed home made ice cream and cake. Uncle Guy was the only one in the neighborhood who had an icehouse and a freezer. Stores didn't sell ice cream then so it was always a real treat.

Uncle Guy planned another treat for Hazel—a buggy ride in his two-seated buggy. He hitched his team to the two-seater and away he went with his four nieces. Driving first to Freeland, he tied the horses to a hitching post in front of Frank Lewis' store. Kittie always had a fear of horses though she'd been brought up with gentle old nags like old Nell. So she got out and waited on the sidewalk. Runaway horses were not all unusual and she wasn't going to risk her neck in any old runaway.

Soon Uncle Guy came out with bulky sacks in both hands—peanuts in

one, candy in the other. Uncle Guy always was partial to sweets.

Wenonah Beach and Riverside Park were about the only places with recreational attractions, but either place would require a whole day—with horses. That left nothing but to ride around on country roads. They rode around a section or two, eating candy and cracking peanuts as they rode. Being girls they found many things to giggle about. So absorbed were they with giggling, eating candy, and munching peanuts that they were unaware of the scenery along the way: Farm houses, barns, rail fences, fields of grain, woods, dirt roads and ditches!

Although they had had a wonderful day—it was one that would bore one to tears today.

Out came the old cart. Without any democratic discussion Hazel and Gertie climbed into the seat, so that automatically made Louise and Kittie horses. They were running up and down the dusty road when Gertie said, "Here comes a buggy. I'm going to get out and hide in that elderberry bush over there." Soon she was hidden from sight. But Hazel sat her ground—looking as proud as a princess when the occupants of the buggy rode by with undisguised smiles and amusement on their faces. It must have looked as incongruous as Pixie and Nixie hauling Yogi Bear in a cart. Gertie wouldn't come out until the buggy had gone some distance. It's doubtful if Louise and Kittie had many rides that day.

One afternoon the girls donned their home made bathing suits. There was none for Hazel so she wore an old cotton dress. The Tittabawassee River was formerly one of the greatest logging streams in Michigan. It had a treacherous bottom—one could be walking along and suddenly drop into a hole. Mother believed in "Safety First." So she accompanied the girls and before they were allowed to go in the water, she tied a rope around each one. And she sat on a big stone near the shore, holding the other ends of the ropes.

The girls would wade out and then flinging themselves on their stomachs would paddle in, dog fashion, with Mother pulling on the ropes. With her cotton dress clinging to her as tight as her skin Hazel looked a perfect Venus. Anyone going up or down the river must have wondered what kind of bait the fisher woman was using, and what fantastic-looking fish she was hauling in. In later years, on her annual October visits Hazel always had to relate these last two experiences.

Then a big day was planned for her benefit—a trip to Wenonah Beach near Bay City, about twenty miles away—and a team to get them there and back again in a day! Father borrowed Uncle Guy's two-seated carriage, putting in a third seat. One of those good picnic dinners was stowed away and the merrymakers piled in: Uncle Herbert, Aunt Mary, Father, Mother, and the four girls.

All went well until within a short distance of Bay City the spring on one end of a seat broke, letting that end down until it rested on the frame of the carriage. The girls were then assigned the broken seat. Going through Bay City they made quite a spectacle with all the girls leaning towards the North Pole. (As funny as the time our car was towed behind the camp trailer with some of the kids riding on the trailer as we rode into St. Ignace.)

They arrived at the Beach in grand style with none of the eight souls lost by the wayside. It would have taken more than a lopsided ride to dampen the girls' spirits.

Wenonah Park must have been in the predevelopment stage—no attractions there but some boats. There were scrubby trees and underbrush and that big expanse of water. Dinner was spread on the ground and relished as much as at a banquet table. After waiting awhile for their food to "settle" they went behind some bushes and soon emerged as full-fledged bathers. The bathing suits were the homespun variety—long full woolen bloomers fastened to an underwaist, and a full skirted woolen dress.

Some other Freeland friends were in the party and Mrs. Etta Sarle, a very tall, large woman about Mother's age, went into the water clad in a tight-waisted, full-skirted cotton wrapper—a long house dress in vogue at the time. When she stood in the water, there was nothing to guess at. Her birthday suit couldn't have shown her off to much better advantage.

While they were splashing and paddling in the water, a man came and said the children would have to go to the bathhouse to dress. Aunt Mary was always ripe for an argument with anyone and she said, "They look a lot more decent than those women in bathing suits." He admitted they did but pointing to Mrs. Sarle said, "Does that woman look decent in that dress?" They argued back and forth and then Aunt Mary grabbed some of the children's clothes and he grabbed some, too. Pros and cons continued for some time but the upshot of it all was that their folks paid the required fee and the children dressed in the bathhouse. That gave them quite a ritzy feeling.

The other memorable event was a baptismal ceremony out near the dock. A group of girls in white dresses stood in the water and another group stood on the dock singing hymns. The minister put them under the water one by one and up they came spitting out water and looking cold. During the ceremony one side of the dock broke away letting several onlookers down into the water unexpectedly. They couldn't be sent to the bathhouse to dress because they didn't have any extra clothes with them. This service made a lasting impression on the girls.

The broken seat having been propped up temporarily, the octet reached home tired but none the worse for their exciting day. No doubt Aunt Mary regretted losing the argument.

The folks decided to go blackberrying with their old crowd—about five couples. They went up near Averill and camped overnight. Uncle Guy promised to look after the girls and Nero was there to guard them. For a change Gertie took Louise in her care and they slept in the front bedroom. Kittie slept with Hazel and felt quite well protected as size counted with her rather than age.

In the night Kittie awoke to find a bad thunderstorm in progress. The lightning was blinding and the thunder deafening. Hazel was sound asleep but Kittie woke her up and asked, "Are you afraid, Hazel?" "Well, I wasn't until you woke me up," she replied. Uncle Guy said he came over in the night to see how they were doing, but finding everything dark and quiet, he judged they were all right and didn't disturb them. Morning found the female quartet safe and cheerful and raring to go again!

Night brought the weary berry pickers home with pails of wild blackberries—some to be eaten fresh and the rest to be canned. Best of all they were glad to find their darlings unmolested and safe.

Every day was filled with fun and excitement and all too soon Hazel's visit came to the end. The girls were loathe to have her leave. Her tomboyish ways had been equal to theirs. Having dreaded her arrival they now dreaded her departure. She left with a promise that Gertie and Kittie would visit her the next summer—a promise that was fulfilled when they spent two weeks in Grand Ledge, Lansing, and Wacousta the summer of 1904—the summer Floyd and Ina were married. Before they went, Floyd said to Kittie, "I want you back before the 23rd of August so you can play *Hearts And Flowers* at my wedding. He had bought this sheet music sometime before. Kittie had mastered it and would be ready.

NOTES

The Lewis Store was on Main Street near the Washington Street intersection. This Lewis was no relative to the Lewis family.

Wenonah Beach was a resort park in Bay City located near the Saginaw River. Families from rural areas would come to the park to spend a pleasurable afternoon. They would swim, picnic, and ride on the amusement rides. However, during Kittie's visit, the amusement rides had not yet been installed.

While the family was at Wenonah, they witnessed a baptism in the Saginaw River. The Baptist and Methodist Episcopal denominations in East Saginaw had been baptizing in the Saginaw River since 1858. Also, the Tittabawassee Township Methodist Episcopal Church had been baptizing in the Tittabawassee River since at least 1857.

Chapter 33

Eggs and Wedding Dresses

The old nag was going full speed but the drunken driver was lashing her over the back, urging her to accelerate her speed. His egg crates were tipping crazily as he drove up and down those gullies. "He's going to lose some of his eggs before he goes much farther," said Mother as she and Aunt Mary met him on their way to Freeland.

Going home from school the three girls came upon a strange sight in Uncle Guy's gully. Egg crates had rolled down the embankment and had been caught by some scrubby-looking shrubs. It appeared that many of them were in fairly good condition. Kittie said, "Let's get some baskets and come and get these eggs." "I don't want the rotten things," said Louise.

Changing her school dress, Kittie grabbed the first old dress she could get her hands on which turned out to be one of Gertie's, several sizes too big for her. It had a big flounce on the bottom and came down to her ankles. But she didn't notice that because her eyes were on those eggs.

Snatching the sturdy egg basket, off she dashed up the road leaving a dusty trail in her wake as evidence of her breakneck speed. She must get those eggs before someone else did!

Filling her basket with unbroken eggs, she scrambled up the embankment stepping on the long flounce in the process. Just then Lucy Haviland came along and Kittie told her she wanted Louise to come, too, but she had turned down the invitation. Lucy saw Mother and Aunt Mary in Freeland and related the episode. Aunt Mary was angry to think Louise wasn't getting any of those eggs.

Uncle Guy had seen the eggs in the gully and had mentally resolved to

gather them at night when he wouldn't be seen. But "The early bird catches the worm." He stood out in the yard and called, "What are you doing?" "Gathering eggs!" Kittie shouted back in a high, staccato voice, without slackening her pace. Her face the hue of a male turkey's wattles, and her torn flounce going flippity-flop about her ankles, she didn't stop for any conversation.

Kittie and Gertie formed a business partnership—Kittie was the business head and transportation executive; Gertie, the cleaner-upper, inspector and distributing manager.

Egg basket emptied, back for another consignment. Egg yolks, egg shells and dirt tangled with one another so her tedious efforts became more and more laborious, and more exacting as she kept her weather eye on the road for fear the egg man would come back and find her stealing his eggs. She found the old adage "Haste makes waste" applicable. She searched through that golden yolky melee as painstakingly as ever the gold-crazed forty-niners searched for gold nuggets in their find at Sutters Mill.

The blood was nearly bursting through her face, but she was determined to finish those sticky eggs before darkness settled down and before Mother arrived home. Her mental eye could just vision Mother's surprise, but Lucy had spilled the beans!

Each return trip home found additional crocks, pans, and other suitable kitchenware overflowing with the gold mine (gold all right). With systematic performance Gertie had separated sheep from the goats—that is to say, the whole from the cracked eggs. At last count the whole eggs totaled ten dozen and the cracked ones about fifteen dozen—so many they lost count. They kept the whole eggs for a few days in case the egg man came back to recover his

Kittie often would have taken the train to Saginaw and then shopped at Ippel's Dry Goods Store on Court & Michigan Avenues across from the Courthouse. The store carried a large line of dry goods. Women's clothing was not ready made, and everything had to be hand sewn.
lasinski Collection

loss. But instead of the *Last Of The Mohicans,* it was the last of the egg man. He seemed to have vanished in thin air somewhere between here and kingdom come. He had come from Saginaw once a week to buy eggs.

In the days before refrigeration cracked eggs wouldn't keep too long. Boiled eggs, fried, scrambled, poached, deviled, custards, puddings—eggs in all forms graced the breakfast, dinner, and supper table. The family was steeped in eggs from eyebrows to toes. Gertie and Kittie had pretty good opinions of themselves as they found their efforts greatly expanding the family economy.

The eggs were finally sold and the current price being 15 cents per dozen. Kittie's net profits totaled $1.50. Because of her seniority Gertie relinquished all claim to the profits. Kittie's little heart nearly burst with pride. That was more money than a man earned in a day. And—hadn't she furnished the backbone of the family living for some time?

In due time a horse and buggy trip was made to Saginaw over the old dirt road—a day's trip there and return. In Ippel's Dry Goods Store on the corner

Floyd and Ina were married on August 23, 1904. They were happily married and celebrated their 50th Anniversary in 1954. Kittie played the same wedding march in 1904 and 1954. This photo was one of their wedding anniversaries.

of Michigan and Court the money changed hands and Kittie became the proud possessor of enough material, lace, and ribbon for the making of a new dress. Thin white with blue pin dots and a blue sash! Dainty and pretty! This dress Kittie wore on August 23, 1904 as she proudly played on Steckert's old organ the wedding march, which was so popular at the time—*Hearts And Flowers.*

As Myrtle Bateman and Albert Munger preceded Ina Steckert and Floyd down the stairs to the parlor, Grandpa Lewis stood waiting there to unite the latter pair in the holy bonds of matrimony. An elderly couple at that! Ina was 20 and Floyd 21 that April and May respectively. Kittie bemoaned the fact that her back had to be toward the bridal bower as she missed most of the show. She hadn't yet become a teacher with eyes in the back of her head!

Ina wore a white silk blouse with much smocking and faggot stitching and openwork with a high, high collar held in place under the ears and in the back with strips of whalebone. Even on her long neck that collar, fastened in the back, looked tight and uncomfortable. Her skirt was of blue-gray (or blue-blue) material, and when starting on the honeymoon, she wore the accompanying jacket. Myrtle also wore a white blouse and skirt.

A bountiful wedding supper was served, and then all was over. Mother liked Ina and felt that Floyd had married a very nice girl—but he was so young and just starting out in the business world. So upon reaching home she felt a little blue—her first fledgling had flown the nest!

Many years later Aunt Annie told Kittie that Aunt Josie never quite got over the fact that Uncle Guy didn't get any of the eggs since he saw them first. But Uncle Guy never tired of telling about the blue (dress) streak that dashed back and forth past his house with eggs and more eggs. "Children and fools enter where old folks fear to tread."

NOTES

The Steckerts were also a long time Freeland family. A William Steckert farm is shown as east of Garfield Road. This may have been Ina's parents' home where her wedding to Floyd Lewis took place. During this era weddings generally took place in the bride's home. Although Reverend Jacob Lewis had retired from the Congregational Church, he still married the couple in the Steckert home. Kittie played the Steckert organ during the wedding ceremony. When Floyd and Ina celebrated their 50th Anniversary in 1954, Kittie once again played the same wedding march on the organ in Floyd's house.

The egg man from Saginaw apparently made regular trips into Freeland to buy eggs wholesale from local farmers. Then he would have returned to Saginaw to resell them to local grocers or distributors for resale. Most of the Saginaw grocers purchased fresh perishable food such as milk, eggs, and poultry from local farmers.

CHAPTER 34

FLOYD

You may wonder why more hasn't been said about Floyd. Born May 9, 1883 he was nearly nine years older than Kittie. By the time she was old enough to remember very many things, he was going to school in Saginaw. Mother said he began working during the summers on the Pere Marquette Railroad and at age fourteen earned most of his clothes from then on.

He was a precocious child and received a great deal of attention from all the relatives. He talked plainly as a baby and they all laughed at everything he said. He was so attached to Mother that it was almost impossible for anyone else to take care of him. Mother loved dancing—she'd rather dance than eat—so Aunt Josie said she would take care of him and let Mother dance. But it was very little dancing she did that night because he objected so strenuously.

When he was two years old, Father and Mother drove in a cutter to Coleman to visit Aunt Estell (Father's younger sister) and Uncle John Symons. It was a very cold day but Floyd couldn't keep a veil over his face. When they reached home the following day, he said, "More riding." We laughed sometimes and said he had been saying it ever since—he did so love to travel all his life. As a boy, he was always telling all the things he was going to do "when my ship comes in." And he'd say, "Oh, Ma, I wish I had a million dollars." When his ship finally came in, the million dollars were missing! But he got around a lot and seemed to have a zest for living.

One day he took a pillowcase to the woods, climbed high up in a tree and bagged a young squirrel. Upon opening the case to show his young quarry, the squirrel jumped out, ran up Mother and sat on her head. It must have taken her for its native tree. Mother was frightened nearly out of her wits and said, "Don't you ever bring a squirrel in the house again!" So the home never boasted a pet squirrel.

Another day he climbed a high tree and brought home two young crows. He kept one and gave one to Uncle Guy. Sam and Pete they were called. They became very good pets but rather mischievous ones. Sam would follow Mother when she hung out the washing, removing some of the clothespins right behind her.

One time Sam took a 50-cent piece of Floyd's and put it in the wagon out in the barn. He used to hide Floyd's shoelaces and other little things. He was very tame and made noises almost like talking. Sam and Pete used to get together and go on long flights. One day they flew to Freeland, lighting on Mr. McCann's fence posts. That was one flight too many. Some folks can't bear to see any animals around. They were both shot that day, and that ended all Floyd's attempts and aspirations of being a wild animal trainer. He had to be content with a dog, cat, and kittens—of which they usually had plenty.

When Floyd got home from school one night he kept following Mother around. She knew he had something on his mind but didn't want to force the issue. After a while he blurted out, "Ma, something awful happened today. I nearly drowned in the river up by the bridge."

Some of the boys had gone from school down to the Tittabawassee River and Floyd stepped in a deep hole and went down twice. Bert Preston grabbed him but Floyd fought like a tiger and would have pulled Bert under if he hadn't given him a good blow almost knocking Floyd out in order to save his life. He was a pretty docile boy that night. Father decided then and there that he should learn to swim. So he gave him swimming lessons in the old Tittabawassee River.

Floyd was an outstanding student. His teacher, Mr. Smith, taught him extra subjects—geometry, trigonometry, etc. as he excelled in mathematics. He and Albert Munger became chums while quite young. They lived about a mile apart and often met out in the woods. The girls used to see their initials carved on several trees. They decided they'd go to Business College together.

Floyd bought a nice new blue bicycle. The summer he was seventeen he rode his bike to Grand Ledge and Wacousta taking orders for some book—*The Life Of William McKinley.* In this way he earned some money toward his college expenses. By the time he reached home on his bike, he had developed

Floyd almost drowned when he stepped into a deep hole in the river next to the Freeland Bridge but he was rescued by his chums. This is the second Freeland Bridge built in 1895. Rafts and piles from the lumbering days still remained in the Tittabawassee River. Vasold Collection

a bad carbuncle on the palm of his hand, just below the fingers. It was a very nasty sore, and he grew almost delirious with the pain. Dr. Cubbage treated him, and it became necessary to have it lanced.

That fall he and Albert Munger enrolled in Bliss Business College where they studied bookkeeping, typing, shorthand, etc. Upon completion of the course Floyd was very highly recommended. He and Albert secured positions and roomed together at Mrs. Brobst's on North Franklin Street in East Saginaw. They became very attached to each other—a regular David and Jonathan relationship. And the close friendship lasted all through the years.

One spring Kittie wrote Floyd that Mrs. Gould had the prettiest hat that she had ever seen in her millinery shop. How she would like that hat! It was a white chip straw trimmed profusely with lilies-of-the-valley. By the time Floyd came home, Laura Maidment had bought the hat, much to Kittie's disappointment. Floyd was real disappointed because he told Mother he fully

Floyd roomed on North Franklin Street in East Saginaw so that he could attend the Bliss Business College. The business college shown here changed names and owners several times, but basic business courses were always offered. The school eventually became the Saginaw Business Institute and today is the Great Lakes Junior College of Business. Ederer Collection

intended to buy that hat. Mother said it was a good thing Laura bought it, as it was much too heavy looking for Kittie's small face. To this day Kittie remembers how that hat looked. "A thing of beauty is a joy forever."

Floyd and Albert usually came home on the train over the weekend. They belonged to the same Sunday school class and went to weekend parties. By this time he was noticing Ina.

Our mare, Fannie, had a beautiful colt, Maude. Floyd broke this colt when she was old enough because he wanted a nice, sleek fast horse to drive over to Steckerts' house. She became a beautiful well-trained horse, but Mother used to worry at first when he was out late at night with Maude because she was so full of life and rather skittish.

Floyd was a good-looking young man with beautiful wavy hair. He was a wonderful vocalist, had lots of dash and could have gone with any of the girls. There was one thing he never could stand—being teased about a girl! Kittie

This photo of Floyd Lewis was taken when he attended Business College and then married in 1904. Kittie always said, "He was a good-looking young man with wavy hair."

began to tease him when he started going with girls, and he hated it so. He had always been very fond of his little sister. But one day he said, "Ma, Kittie is getting to be the meanest little thing!"

Mother thought Ina was so good to and responsible for her three young brothers that she would make a good wife. Floyd asked Mother about her choice of girls and she said, "Well, there's Ina Steckert—I think she's a nice girl." He thought so, too, and as you know, sometime later he led her to the altar to the tune of wedding bells. They went to the St. Louis Exposition, St. Louis, Missouri, on August 23, 1904 on their honeymoon.

NOTES

Albert Munger lived about a mile from Floyd's home. There is a Wells Munger farm between the farms of Charles Foote and Peter Doran on Pierce Road. This is probably the home where Albert Munger lived. It would be a short distance from the Lewis farms.The bridge where Floyd almost drowned would have been the Freeland Bridge built in 1870 over the river on Washington Street or Freeland Road. It was rebuilt in 1895.

Fred H. Bliss had established business schools in New England and throughout Michigan before he established the International Business College at Baum & Tuscola Streets in the Cass House, East Saginaw, in 1885. Students came from all over the state to attend this well run college. Business courses in penmanship, letter writing, business papers, rapid calculations, and bookkeeping were taught. Students roomed in nearby boarding houses or hotels. This is the school that Floyd and Albert would have attended.

Francis R. Alger graduated from one of the Bliss Colleges in 1906. He married Fred's daughter, Madge Bliss. Then Alger and Fred H. Bliss opened the Bliss-Alger Business College and School of Shorthand in 1907 in the Brewer Block, 127 North Franklin Street in East Saginaw. The International Business College and Bliss-Alger Business College merged in 1911 becoming one of Michigan's largest business colleges. In 1929 it became the Detroit Business Institute. In 1957 the Davenport Schools purchased it, renaming it the Saginaw Business Institute. In 1985 it became the Great Lakes Junior College of Business and has moved from its downtown Saginaw location to a spacious campus on Bay Road. Students from all over Michigan attend the business college today.

Floyd had a successful business career. He and Ina lived in Midland where he worked and they raised their family—Kathryn, Cleone, Lella Mae, and Alan. Floyd and Ina shared many happy years together and were fortunate to celebrate their 50th wedding anniversary.

Kittie and all her students at the one-room Law School on Buck Road have posed outside their schoolhouse in 1911. Kittie is standing in the back row. This was 20-year-old Kittie's first teaching position. She taught 44 pupils for $46 per month and was paid an extra $1 to do the general maintenance. She taught at Law School until 1918.

Right, Kittie as a young woman in her twenties.

EPILOGUE

Kittie attended the old two-story frame Freeland schoolhouse through her tenth grade. Then she completed her eleventh and twelfth grades at Arthur Hill High School at Court & Harrison Streets in Saginaw, graduating in 1909. The Freeland School ended with the tenth grade. Kittie then took teacher's education classes in the County Normal off campus program through Central Michigan College. This Teacher's Certificate allowed her to teach in Freeland.

When she was 20 in 1911, Kittie began teaching in the one-room Law School on Buck Road for $46 a month. She taught 44 pupils in all eight grades. Some students were almost her same age. She was paid an extra $1 per month to do the janitorial work of keeping the pot-bellied stove well stoked with wood or coal, washing and cleaning blackboards, sweeping, and general cleaning and maintenance.

In 1918 she taught school at the one-room Vasold School across the Tittabawassee River from her home at 360 South Main Street. She had to row one-half mile down the river, dock the boat, and then walk another one-half mile across fields to the school each morning. Often times her father would row her across the river going to school and coming back home again. She walked over the frozen river in the winter months.

Kittie often took the Pere Marquette Train to Saginaw's Potter Street Station so she could spend the day with Gertie, shopping, visiting, and enjoying "plays" at the Franklin or Mecca Theatres. She and her parents also took the train to Midland to visit her brother Floyd and Ina Lewis. Telephones and automobiles were not commonly used in Freeland in 1919, and Kittie walked to school and wherever she needed to go.

The United States had entered into World War I in 1917. Liberty Bonds, today's equivalency of Savings Bonds, were sold to help finance the War. Kittie was proud to purchase these Bonds, buying $225 worth in 1919 with her wages. The Women's Suffrage Movement was supported with Amendments and President Wilson's historic speech in 1918. Michigan was the first state in granting voting rights to women. Kittie was the first woman in Tittabawassee Township to register on February 12 and vote in a primary election on March 5, 1919.

The flu epidemic of 1918-1919 was at its peak, and her one-room Vasold School was closed often in the winter and then fumigated. Her pupil attendance was very low. Several people in Freeland died of the flu. Kittie played the organ or piano at their many funerals and for her favorite Uncle Guy while he was ill with heart problems. He died on March 9, 1919. Kittie and her friends often entertained in each other's homes, singing and playing the piano, organ, and other musical instruments.

In 1919 Kittie accepted a Primary Department position at the Freeland School on Church Street for $75 per month. She taught 57 students in the first four grades. Only two other teachers taught all other grades. When fire destroyed part of the school building in the 1920s, Kittie taught in the Congregational Church dining room, while other classes were held in the Church auditorium and the Maccabee Hall until the brick school was rebuilt.

As Kittie always said "My loves either came too early or too late," so she never married. She dearly loved babies and small children, and always talked about having her own family some day. However, she became an educator, a substitute mother, and an inspiration to hundreds of Freeland children throughout her 48-year teaching career. For several years she was chairman of the Preschool Clinic and Summer Roundup and personally called at each home to explain the program and recruit youngsters for the session. From 1945 until she retired in May 1959, she taught the kindergarten classes at the Freeland School. At her retirement party, the children presented her with a $132.65 gift. The faculty gave her a Royal Holland Pewter Tea Service.

Kittie had always been active in the Saginaw County Teachers Club, now known as the Michigan Education Association. As a member, she had written Study Units, been its representative to the Kellogg Foundation School System, served as a Helping Teacher for Tittabawassee Township Schools, trained the intermediate grades who participated in the May Music Festival at Saginaw's Auditorium, served as a delegate to the National Education Association Convention in Los Angeles, and been invited to teach in the Owosso and Mt. Pleasant kindergarten classes.

Gertie married her high school sweetheart, William Ray Olmsted, on September 16, 1911.

Her family also shared Kittie's great love for education. Before her mother, Katie Allen, married Watson Lewis in 1882, she also taught at the Law and Vasold one-room schools. Gertie taught for a year before she married William Ray Olmsted in 1911. Her children—Helen, Sherman, and Virginia—all became educators. Kittie's grandfather, Jacob Lewis, was Tittabawassee Township's first teacher when he arrived in 1854.

Louise Allen was Kittie's and Gertie's best friend and double cousin. The three-some engaged in many childhood experiences together. Louise became a music teacher. Sadly, she died of exhaustion on May 18, 1913. She was only 22 years old.

Gertrude and William Ray Olmsted were high school sweethearts. On one occasion while they were courting, they took a ride down the Tittabawassee River in a flat bottom rowboat. It became dark before they could return, and they couldn't find their way back. So they just remained sitting in their rowboat on the river the entire night. Gertie recounted the story several times throughout her life in spite of the gossip it may have created at the time. They married soon after on September 16, 1911, and they remained happily married for 64 years.

Gertie brought her children to visit the folks back home. Shown from left to right: Kittie, Gertie, Watson holding Louise, and Katie with Virginia standing in front of her.

Ray's work as a mechanical engineer took him to Saginaw where he worked for Jackson & Church Company. They made their home in East Saginaw where they raised their four children—Virginia, Louise, Helen, and Sherman.

Gertie and Kittie remained good friends their entire life. Gertie brought her children whenever she visited Kittie, and they always reminisced about their childhood days. It was Virginia who was fascinated with their tales, and she urged Kittie to write her stories in a book. Kittie did so after she retired in 1959. She spent her days at her ancient black manual typewriter, typing out her stories after she had first handwritten them.

Rose Dill and Kittie were good friends, and they both belonged to the American Bell Association. They collected bells from all over the world. They both flew for the first time when they attended a Bell Association convention in San Francisco, California. Kittie was attracted to colorful glass vases as a

Gertie and Kittie took several trips together. They are shown here—Gertie on the left and Kittie and her dog on the right—at Grindstone City.

young child. She also kept a large collection of vases and pitchers, numbering and writing a history for each one.

Kittie bought a new car but never learned to drive it. Her father drove the car taking the family and Gertie's family along on camping trips. The car trips ended when Watson became blind and then died in 1944. Gertie and Kittie often took trips together.

Kittie's parents allowed her to take piano lessons only if she shared her musical talents with others. Kittie kept that promise throughout her life. She played for weddings, funerals, and home entertainments. Kittie served as Sunday school teacher, clerk, treasurer, organist, and pianist for the Freeland Congregational Church for over 50 years. When this church disbanded, she joined the Freeland Baptist Church and shared her musical talents there. She later bought an electric organ for her own personal enjoyment.

Longevity seemed to favor the Lewis family. Her grandfather, Jacob Lewis,

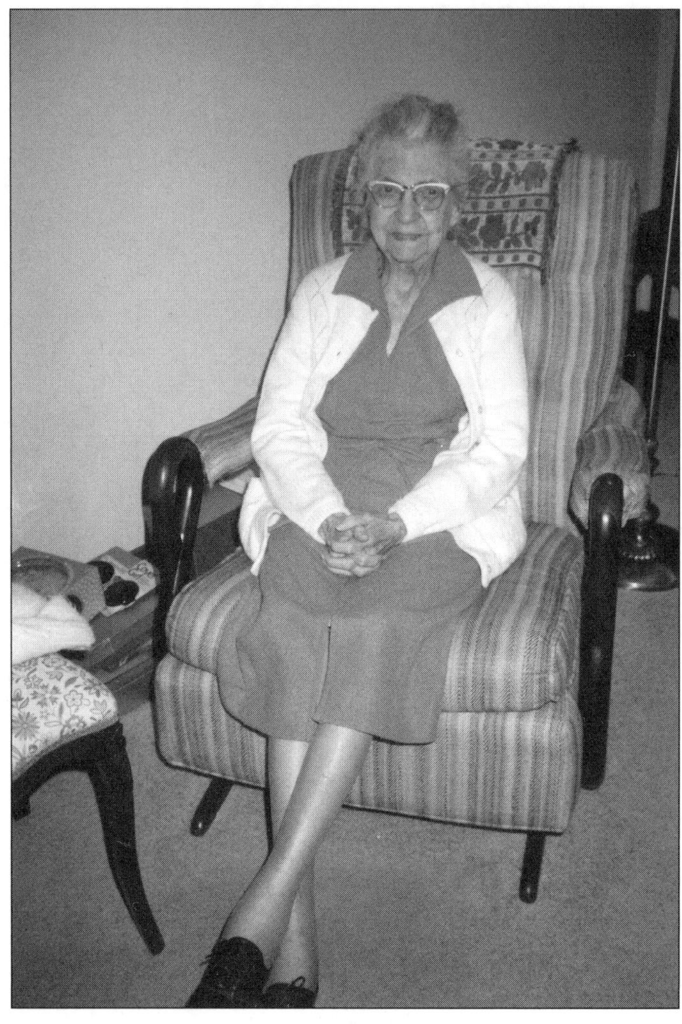

Gertie lived to be 101 years old and spent her final years at St. Francis Home. Photo of Gertie Olmsted in her 90s.

outlived three wives and died at age 96. Kittie cared for her mother, Katie Lewis, who became blind and deaf, at their home until she died in 1956 at age 95. Kittie continued to live at the family home at 360 S. Main Street until the house was sold when she entered the Hoyt Nursing Home in Saginaw several years prior to her death in 1985. Although Kittie suffered from osteoporosis and glaucoma, she happily entertained the Home's residents with her piano music after dinner. Gertie visited her daily. Kittie was 93 and was buried next to her

Kittie spent her last years at the Hoyt Nursing Home in Saginaw. She is seen here at Hoyt Nursing Home. She lived to age 93.

parents in Freeland's Pine Grove Cemetery. Gertie spent her last remaining years at the St. Francis Home in Saginaw where she died in 1989 at 101 years of age. Gertie's daughter, Louise McPhee, was 92 when she died in 2007. And Virginia? Oh, yes! Ninety-four year old Virginia happily celebrates her half-century of birthdays yearly at her assisted-living residence in Tucson, Arizona! And she enjoys reading Kittie's Memoirs and reminiscing with each passing year!

Watson and Katie Lewis at their home at 360 S. Main Street during the early 1940s.

Watson, Katie, and Kittie Lewis left the farm on Midland & Pierce Roads and moved to this house at 360 South Main Street in the Freeland Village in 1918. Kittie lived in the home until it was sold when she moved to the Hoyt Nursing Home.

Family Photo Album

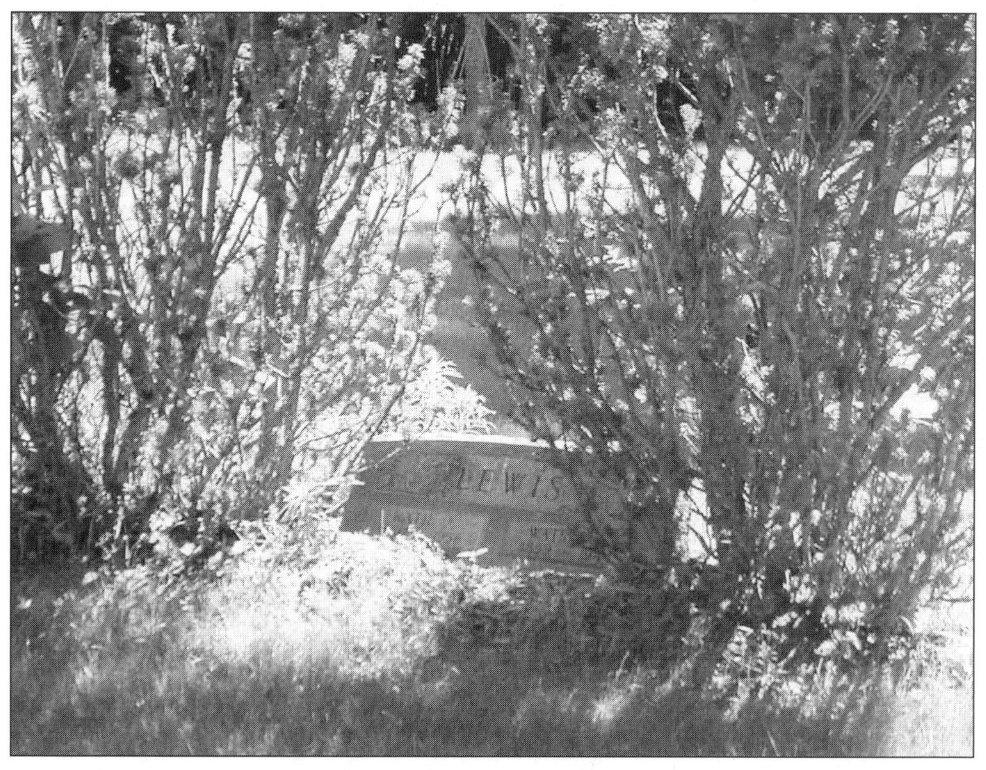

The Watson and Katie Lewis graves at Pine Grove Cemetery. Kittie's unmarked grave is nearby.

Gertie's children—Louise, Helen, and Virginia—in 1917.

Gertie's son, Sherman Olmsted, in February 1921.

Virginia and Louise Olmsted in their Saginaw neighborhood, about 1917.

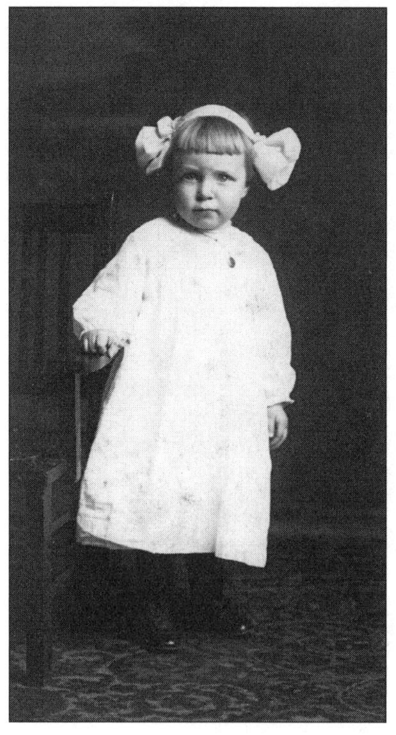

Above, Louise, Helen, and Virginia visiting Auntie, Watson and Katie Lewis at their Freeland home, about 1920.

Left, Virginia Claire Olmsted's birthday card to Aunt Kathryn on December 8, 1914.

Virginia Olmsted at her high school graduation in 1930.

Virginia and her husband, Malcolm Cutler, in November 1975.

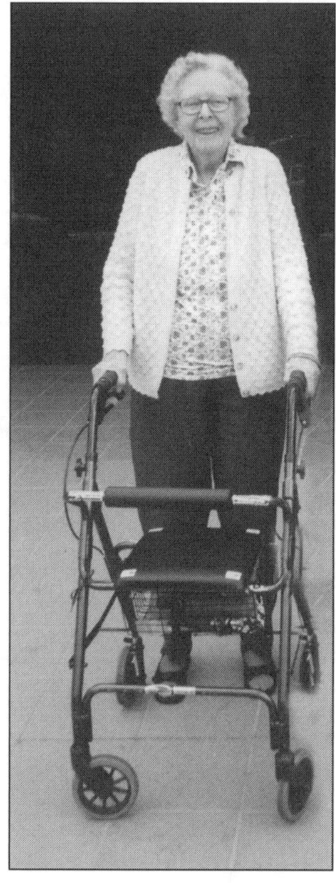

Virginia today at her Assisted-Living Residence in Arizona.

The Watson Lewis Family posed for the photographer about 1943. From left to right: Floyd, Katie, Ina, Watson, Kittie, Louise Olmsted McPhee, Gertie, and William Ray Olmsted.

Jacob H. Lewis and his children, grandchildren, and great-grandchildren have gathered for this Lewis Family reunion in 1917. Adults sitting from left to right: William H. Lewis, Katie A. Lewis, Watson A. Lewis holding Louise Olmsted, Jacob H. Lewis (long beard), Mary Lewis Allen, Herbert L. Allen, Cora Lewis. Grandchildren standing from left to right: William R. Olmsted holding Helen, Gertie Olmsted, Floyd Lewis, Kittie Lewis, Ina Lewis. Next could be William H. Lewis' four children with their spouses—Winnie, Leon, Arthur, Willie and Florence Lewis' son—Earl Symons. The boy standing and the children sitting in the front would be the great-grandchildren—the children of those couples, standing in the back. Virginia Olmsted is the first girl from left, sitting in front of Katie.

For Additional Copies of:

Growing up on the Banks of the

Mighty Tittabawassee

Please Send $19.95, plus $1.20 Tax and
$4.00 Shipping and Handing,
or a total of $25.15 to:

Thomastown Publishing Co.
P. O. Box 6471
Saginaw, MI 48608-6471
E-Mail: Ttpublishing@aol.com

Please allow two weeks for delivery